William Shakespeare (bapt. 26 April 1564 – 23 April 1616) was an English poet, playwright and actor, widely regarded as the greatest writer in the English language and the world's greatest dramatist. He is often called England's national poet and the "Bard of Avon". His extant works, including collaborations, consist of approximately 39 plays, 154 sonnets, two long narrative poems, and a few other verses, some of uncertain authorship. His plays have been translated into every major living language and are performed more often than those of any other playwright. Shakespeare was born and raised in Stratford-upon-Avon, Warwickshire. At the age of 18, he married Anne Hathaway, with whom he had three children: Susanna and twins Hamnet and Judith. Sometime between 1585 and 1592, he began a successful career in London as an actor, writer, and part-owner of a playing company called the Lord Chamberlain's Men, later known as the King's Men. At age 49 (around 1613), he appears to have retired to Stratford, where he died three years later. (Source: Wikipedia)

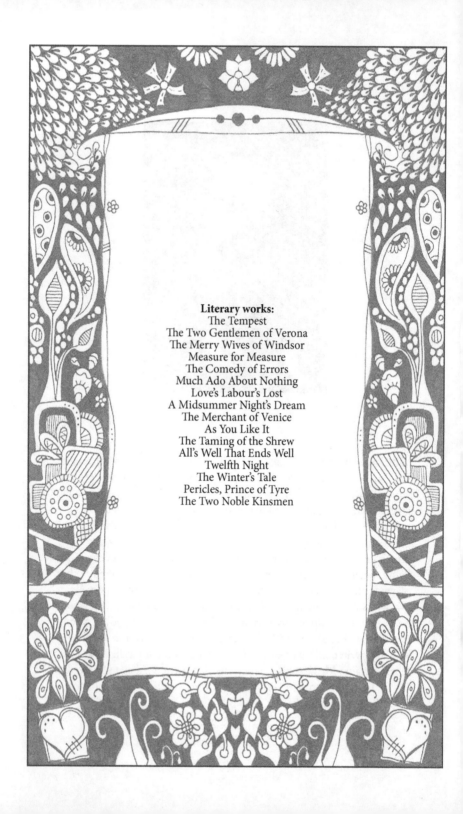

Literary works:
The Tempest
The Two Gentlemen of Verona
The Merry Wives of Windsor
Measure for Measure
The Comedy of Errors
Much Ado About Nothing
Love's Labour's Lost
A Midsummer Night's Dream
The Merchant of Venice
As You Like It
The Taming of the Shrew
All's Well That Ends Well
Twelfth Night
The Winter's Tale
Pericles, Prince of Tyre
The Two Noble Kinsmen

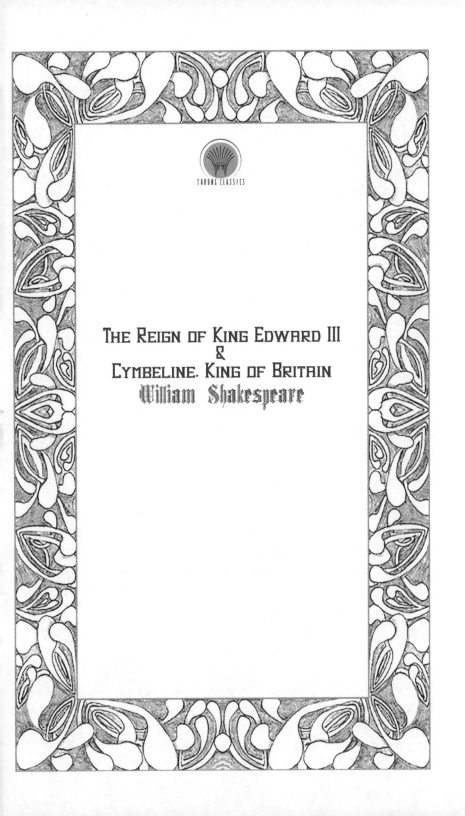

THRONE CLASSICS

THE REIGN OF KING EDWARD III
&
CYMBELINE, KING OF BRITAIN
William Shakespeare

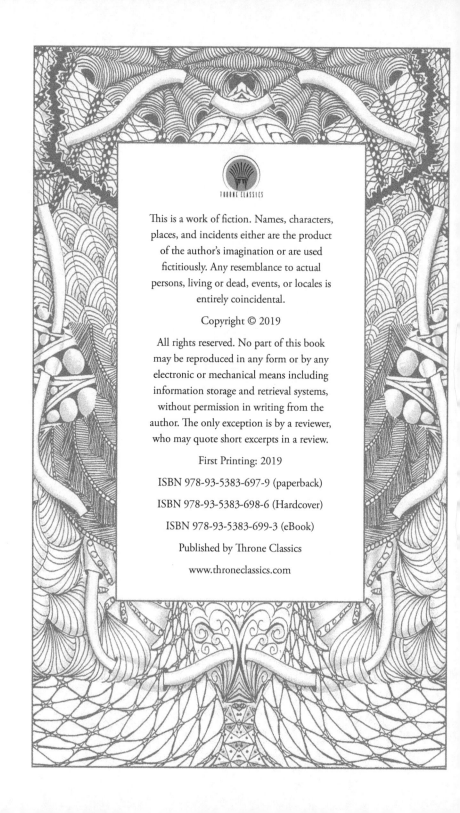

Copyright © 2019

First Printing: 2019

ISBN 978-93-5383-697-9 (paperback)

ISBN 978-93-5383-698-6 (Hardcover)

ISBN 978-93-5383-699-3 (eBook)

Published by Throne Classics

www.throneclassics.com

Contents

The Reign of King Edward III
&
Cymbeline, King of Britain

THE REIGN OF KING EDWARD III

PERSONS REPRESENTED.

EDWARD THE THIRD, King of England.

EDWARD, Prince of Wales, his Son.

Earl of WARWICK.

Earl of DERBY.

Earl of SALISBURY.

Lord AUDLEY.

Lord PERCY.

LODOWICK, Edward's Confident.

Sir WILLIAM MOUNTAGUE.

Sir JOHN COPLAND.

Two ESQUIRES, and a HERALD, English.

ROBERT, styling himself Earl, of Artois.

Earl of MONTFORT, and

GOBIN DE GREY.

JOHN, King of France.

CHARLES, and PHILIP, his Sons.

Duke of LORRAIN.

VILLIERS, a French Lord.

King of BOHEMIA, Aid to King John.

A POLISH CAPTAIN, Aid to King John.

Six CITIZENS of Calais.

A CAPTAIN, and

A POOR INHABITANT, of the same.

Another CAPTAIN.

A MARINER.

Three HERALDS; and

Four other FRENCHMEN.

DAVID, King of Scotland.

Earl DOUGLAS; and

Two MESSENGERS, Scotch.

PHILIPPA, Edward's Queen.

Countess of SALISBURY.

A FRENCH WOMAN.

Lords, and divers other Attendants; Heralds, Officers, Soldiers, &c.

Scene, dispers'd; in England, Flanders, and France.

ACT I.

SCENE I. London. A Room of State in the Palace. Flourish.

[Enter King Edward, Derby, Prince Edward, Audley, and Artois.]

KING EDWARD.

Robert of Artois, banished though thou be

>From France, thy native Country, yet with us

Thou shalt retain as great a Seigniorie:

For we create thee Earl of Richmond here.

And now go forwards with our pedigree:

Who next succeeded Phillip le Bew?

ARTOIS.

Three sons of his, which all successfully

Did sit upon their father's regal Throne,

Yet died, and left no issue of their loins.

KING EDWARD.

But was my mother sister unto those?

ARTOIS.

She was, my Lord; and only Isabel

Was all the daughters that this Phillip had,

Whom afterward your father took to wife;

And from the fragrant garden of her womb

Your gracious self, the flower of Europe's hope,

Derived is inheritor to France.

But note the rancor of rebellious minds:

When thus the lineage of le Bew was out,

The French obscured your mother's Privilege,

And, though she were the next of blood, proclaimed

John, of the house of Valois, now their king:

The reason was, they say, the Realm of France,

Replete with Princes of great parentage,

Ought not admit a governor to rule,

Except he be descended of the male;

And that's the special ground of their contempt,

Wherewith they study to exclude your grace:

But they shall find that forged ground of theirs

To be but dusty heaps of brittle sand.

Perhaps it will be thought a heinous thing,

That I, a French man, should discover this;

But heaven I call to record of my vows:

It is not hate nor any private wrong,

But love unto my country and the right,

Provokes my tongue, thus lavish in report.

You are the lineal watchman of our peace,

And John of Valois indirectly climbs;

What then should subjects but embrace their King?

Ah, where in may our duty more be seen,

Than striving to rebate a tyrant's pride

And place the true shepherd of our commonwealth?

KING EDWARD.

This counsel, Artois, like to fruitful showers,

Hath added growth unto my dignity;

And, by the fiery vigor of thy words,

Hot courage is engendered in my breast,

Which heretofore was raked in ignorance,

But now doth mount with golden wings of fame,

And will approve fair Isabel's descent,

Able to yoke their stubborn necks with steel,

That spurn against my sovereignty in France.

        [Sound a horn.]

A messenger?—Lord Audley, know from whence.

        [Exit Audley, and returns.]

AUDLEY.

The Duke of Lorrain, having crossed the seas,

Entreats he may have conference with your highness.

KING EDWARD.

Admit him, Lords, that we may hear the news.

   [Exeunt Lords. King takes his State. Re-enter Lords; with Lorrain, attended.]

Say, Duke of Lorrain, wherefore art thou come?

LORRAIN.

The most renowned prince, King John of France,

Doth greet thee, Edward, and by me commands,

That, for so much as by his liberal gift

The Guyen Dukedom is entailed to thee,

Thou do him lowly homage for the same.

And, for that purpose, here I summon thee,

Repair to France within these forty days,

That there, according as the custom is,

Thou mayst be sworn true liegeman to our King;

Or else thy title in that province dies,

And he him self will repossess the place.

KING EDWARD.

See, how occasion laughs me in the face!

No sooner minded to prepare for France,

But straight I am invited,—nay, with threats,

Upon a penalty, enjoined to come:

Twere but a childish part to say him nay.—

Lorrain, return this answer to thy Lord:

I mean to visit him as he requests;

But how? not servilely disposed to bend,

But like a conqueror to make him bow.

His lame unpolished shifts are come to light;

And truth hath pulled the vizard from his face,

That set a gloss upon his arrogance.

Dare he command a fealty in me?

Tell him, the Crown that he usurps, is mine,

And where he sets his foot, he ought to kneel.

Tis not a petty Dukedom that I claim,

But all the whole Dominions of the Realm;

Which if with grudging he refuse to yield,

I'll take away those borrowed plumes of his,

And send him naked to the wilderness.

LORRAIN.

Then, Edward, here, in spite of all thy Lords,

I do pronounce defiance to thy face.

PRINCE EDWARD.

Defiance, French man? we rebound it back,

Even to the bottom of thy master's throat.

And, be it spoke with reverence of the King,

My gracious father, and these other Lords,

I hold thy message but as scurrilous,

And him that sent thee, like the lazy drone,

Crept up by stealth unto the Eagle's nest;

>From whence we'll shake him with so rough a storm,

As others shall be warned by his harm.

WARWICK.

Bid him leave of the Lyons case he wears,

Least, meeting with the Lyon in the field,

He chance to tear him piecemeal for his pride.

ARTOIS.

The soundest counsel I can give his grace,

Is to surrender ere he be constrained.

A voluntary mischief hath less scorn,

Than when reproach with violence is borne.

LORRAIN.

Degenerate Traitor, viper to the place

Where thou was fostered in thine infancy,

Bearest thou a part in this conspiracy?

[He draws his sword.]

KING EDWARD.

Lorrain, behold the sharpness of this steel:

[Drawing his.]

Fervent desire that sits against my heart,

Is far more thorny pricking than this blade;

That, with the nightingale, I shall be scared,

As oft as I dispose my self to rest,

Until my colours be displayed in France:

This is my final Answer; so be gone.

LORRAIN.

It is not that, nor any English brave,

Afflicts me so, as doth his poisoned view,

That is most false, should most of all be true.

[Exeunt Lorrain, and Train.]

KING EDWARD.

Now, Lord, our fleeting Bark is under sail;

Our gage is thrown, and war is soon begun,

But not so quickly brought unto an end.

[Enter Mountague.]

But wherefore comes Sir William Mountague?

How stands the league between the Scot and us?

MOUNTAGUE.

Cracked and dissevered, my renowned Lord.

The treacherous King no sooner was informed

Of your with drawing of your army back,

But straight, forgetting of his former oath,

He made invasion on the bordering Towns:

Barwick is won, Newcastle spoiled and lost,

And now the tyrant hath begirt with siege

The Castle of Rocksborough, where inclosed

The Countess Salisbury is like to perish.

KING EDWARD.

That is thy daughter, Warwick, is it not?

Whose husband hath in Brittain served so long

About the planting of Lord Mountford there?

WARWICK.

It is, my Lord.

KING EDWARD.

Ignoble David! hast thou none to grieve

But silly Ladies with thy threatening arms?

But I will make you shrink your snaily horns!

First, therefore, Audley, this shall be thy charge,

Go levy footmen for our wars in France;

And, Ned, take muster of our men at arms:

In every shire elect a several band.

Let them be Soldiers of a lusty spirit,

Such as dread nothing but dishonor's blot;

Be wary, therefore, since we do commence

A famous War, and with so mighty a nation.

Derby, be thou Ambassador for us

Unto our Father in Law, the Earl of Henalt:

Make him acquainted with our enterprise,

And likewise will him, with our own allies

That are in Flanders, to solicit to

The Emperour of Almaigne in our name.

My self, whilst you are jointly thus employed,

Will, with these forces that I have at hand,

March, and once more repulse the traitorous Scot.

But, Sirs, be resolute: we shall have wars

On every side; and, Ned, thou must begin

Now to forget thy study and thy books,

And ure thy shoulders to an Armor's weight.

PRINCE EDWARD.

As cheerful sounding to my youthful spleen

This tumult is of war's increasing broils,

As, at the Coronation of a king,

The joyful clamours of the people are,

When Ave, Caesar! they pronounce aloud.

Within this school of honor I shall learn

Either to sacrifice my foes to death,

Or in a rightful quarrel spend my breath.

Then cheerfully forward, each a several way;

In great affairs tis nought to use delay.

[Exeunt.]

SCENE II. Roxborough. Before the Castle.

[Enter the Countess.]

COUNTESS.

Alas, how much in vain my poor eyes gaze

For succour that my sovereign should send!

Ah, cousin Mountague, I fear thou wants

The lively spirit, sharply to solicit

With vehement suit the king in my behalf:

Thou dost not tell him, what a grief it is

To be the scornful captive of a Scot,

Either to be wooed with broad untuned oaths,

Or forced by rough insulting barbarism;

Thou doest not tell him, if he here prevail,

How much they will deride us in the North,

And, in their wild, uncivil, skipping gigs,

Bray forth their Conquest and our overthrow

Even in the barren, bleak, and fruitless air.

[Enter David and Douglas, Lorrain.]

I must withdraw, the everlasting foe

Comes to the wall; I'll closely step aside,

And list their babble, blunt and full of pride.

KING DAVID.

My Lord of Lorrain, to our brother of France

Commend us, as the man in Christendom

That we most reverence and entirely love.

Touching your embassage, return and say,

That we with England will not enter parley,

Nor never make fair weather, or take truce;

But burn their neighbor towns, and so persist

With eager Rods beyond their City York.

And never shall our bonny riders rest,

Nor rusting canker have the time to eat

Their light borne snaffles nor their nimble spurs,

Nor lay aside their Jacks of Gymould mayle,

Nor hang their staves of grained Scottish ash

In peaceful wise upon their City walls,

Nor from their buttoned tawny leathern belts

Dismiss their biting whinyards, till your King

Cry out: Enough, spare England now for pity!

Farewell, and tell him that you leave us here

Before this Castle; say, you came from us,

Even when we had that yielded to our hands.

LORRAIN.

I take my leave, and fairly will return

Your acceptable greeting to my king.

[Exit Lorrain.]

KING DAVID.

Now, Douglas, to our former task again,

For the division of this certain spoil.

DOUGLAS.

My liege, I crave the Lady, and no more.

KING DAVID.

Nay, soft ye, sir; first I must make my choice,

And first I do bespeak her for my self.

DOUGLAS.

Why then, my liege, let me enjoy her jewels.

KING DAVID.

Those are her own, still liable to her,

And who inherits her, hath those with all.

[Enter a Scot in haste.]

MESSENGER.

My liege, as we were pricking on the hills,

To fetch in booty, marching hitherward,

We might descry a might host of men;

The Sun, reflecting on the armour, shewed

A field of plate, a wood of picks advanced.

Bethink your highness speedily herein:

An easy march within four hours will bring

The hindmost rank unto this place, my liege.

KING DAVID.

Dislodge, dislodge! it is the king of England.

DOUGLAS.

Jemmy, my man, saddle my bonny black.

KING DAVID.

Meanst thou to fight, Douglas? we are too weak.

DOUGLAS.

I know it well, my liege, and therefore fly.

COUNTESS.

My Lords of Scotland, will ye stay and drink?

KING DAVID.

She mocks at us, Douglas; I cannot endure it.

COUNTESS.

Say, good my Lord, which is he must have the Lady,

And which her jewels? I am sure, my Lords,

Ye will not hence, till you have shared the spoils.

KING DAVID.

She heard the messenger, and heard our talk;

And now that comfort makes her scorn at us.

[Another messenger.]

MESSENGER.

Arm, my good Lord! O, we are all surprised!

COUNTESS.

After the French ambassador, my liege,

And tell him, that you dare not ride to York;

Excuse it that your bonny horse is lame.

KING DAVID.

She heard that too; intolerable grief!

Woman, farewell! Although I do not stay…

[Exeunt Scots.]

COUNTESS.

Tis not for fear, and yet you run away.—

O happy comfort, welcome to our house!

The confident and boisterous boasting Scot,

That swore before my walls they would not back

For all the armed power of this land,

With faceless fear that ever turns his back,

Turned hence against the blasting North-east wind

Upon the bare report and name of Arms.

[Enter Mountague.]

O Summer's day! See where my Cousin comes!

MOUNTAGUE.

How fares my Aunt? We are not Scots;

Why do you shut your gates against your friends?

COUNTESS.

Well may I give a welcome, Cousin, to thee,

For thou comst well to chase my foes from hence.

MOUNTAGUE.

The king himself is come in person hither;

Dear Aunt, descend, and gratulate his highness.

COUNTESS.

How may I entertain his Majesty,

To shew my duty and his dignity?

[Exit, from above.]

[Enter King Edward, Warwick, Artois, with others.]

KING EDWARD.

What, are the stealing Foxes fled and gone,

Before we could uncouple at their heels?

WARWICK.

They are, my liege; but, with a cheerful cry,

Hot hounds and hardy chase them at the heels.

[Enter Countess.]

KING EDWARD.

This is the Countess, Warwick, is it not?

WARWICK.

Even she, my liege; whose beauty tyrants fear,

As a May blossom with pernicious winds,

Hath sullied, withered, overcast, and done.

KING EDWARD.

Hath she been fairer, Warwick, than she is?

WARWICK.

My gracious King, fair is she not at all,

27

If that her self were by to stain her self,

As I have scene her when she was her self.

KING EDWARD.

What strange enchantment lurked in those her eyes,

When they excelled this excellence they have,

That now her dim decline hath power to draw

My subject eyes from persing majesty,

To gaze on her with doting admiration?

COUNTESS.

In duty lower than the ground I kneel,

And for my dull knees bow my feeling heart,

To witness my obedience to your highness,

With many millions of a subject's thanks

For this your Royal presence, whose approach

Hath driven war and danger from my gate.

KING EDWARD.

Lady, stand up; I come to bring thee peace,

How ever thereby I have purchased war.

COUNTESS.

No war to you, my liege; the Scots are gone,

And gallop home toward Scotland with their hate.

KING EDWARD.

Least, yielding here, I pine in shameful love,

Come, we'll pursue the Scots;—Artois, away!

COUNTESS.

A little while, my gracious sovereign, stay,

And let the power of a mighty king

Honor our roof; my husband in the wars,

When he shall hear it, will triumph for joy;

Then, dear my liege, now niggard not thy state:

Being at the wall, enter our homely gate.

KING EDWARD.

Pardon me, countess, I will come no near;

I dreamed to night of treason, and I fear.

COUNTESS.

Far from this place let ugly treason lie!

KING EDWARD.

No farther off, than her conspiring eye,

Which shoots infected poison in my heart,

Beyond repulse of wit or cure of Art.

Now, in the Sun alone it doth not lie,

With light to take light from a mortal eye;

For here two day stars that mine eyes would see

More than the Sun steals mine own light from me,

Contemplative desire, desire to be

In contemplation, that may master thee!

Warwick, Artois, to horse and let's away!

COUNTESS.

What might I speak to make my sovereign stay?

KING EDWARD.

What needs a tongue to such a speaking eye,

That more persuades than winning Oratory?

COUNTESS.

Let not thy presence, like the April sun,

Flatter our earth and suddenly be done.

More happy do not make our outward wall

Than thou wilt grace our inner house withal.

Our house, my liege, is like a Country swain,

Whose habit rude and manners blunt and plain

Presageth nought, yet inly beautified

With bounties, riches and faire hidden pride.

For where the golden Ore doth buried lie,

The ground, undecked with nature's tapestry,

Seems barren, sere, unfertile, fructless, dry;

And where the upper turf of earth doth boast

His pied perfumes and party coloured coat,

Delve there, and find this issue and their pride

To spring from ordure and corruption's side.

But, to make up my all too long compare,

These ragged walls no testimony are,

What is within; but, like a cloak, doth hide

>From weather's Waste the under garnished pride.

More gracious then my terms can let thee be,

Intreat thy self to stay a while with me.

KING EDWARD.

As wise, as fair; what fond fit can be heard,

When wisdom keeps the gate as beauty's guard?—

It shall attend, while I attend on thee:

Come on, my Lords; here will I host to night.

[Exeunt.]

ACT II.

SCENE I. The Same. Gardens of the Castle.

[Enter Lodowick.]

LODOWICK.

I might perceive his eye in her eye lost,

His ear to drink her sweet tongue's utterance,

And changing passion, like inconstant clouds

That rack upon the carriage of the winds,

Increase and die in his disturbed cheeks.

Lo, when she blushed, even then did he look pale,

As if her cheeks by some enchanted power

Attracted had the cherry blood from his:

Anon, with reverent fear when she grew pale,

His cheeks put on their scarlet ornaments;

But no more like her oriental red,

Than Brick to Coral or live things to dead.

Why did he then thus counterfeit her looks?

If she did blush, twas tender modest shame,

Being in the sacred presence of a King;

If he did blush, twas red immodest shame,

To veil his eyes amiss, being a king;

If she looked pale, twas silly woman's fear,

To bear her self in presence of a king;

If he looked pale, it was with guilty fear,

To dote amiss, being a mighty king.

Then, Scottish wars, farewell; I fear twill prove

A lingering English siege of peevish love.

Here comes his highness, walking all alone.

[Enter King Edward.]

KING EDWARD.

She is grown more fairer far since I came hither,

Her voice more silver every word than other,

Her wit more fluent. What a strange discourse

Unfolded she of David and his Scots!

'Even thus', quoth she, 'he spake', and then spoke broad,

With epithites and accents of the Scot,

But somewhat better than the Scot could speak:

'And thus', quoth she, and answered then her self—

For who could speak like her but she her self—

Breathes from the wall an Angel's note from Heaven

Of sweet defiance to her barbarous foes.

When she would talk of peace, me thinks, her tongue

Commanded war to prison; when of war,

It wakened Caesar from his Roman grave,

To hear war beautified by her discourse.

Wisdom is foolishness but in her tongue,

Beauty a slander but in her fair face,

There is no summer but in her cheerful looks,

Nor frosty winter but in her disdain.

I cannot blame the Scots that did besiege her,

For she is all the Treasure of our land;

But call them cowards, that they ran away,

Having so rich and fair a cause to stay.—

Art thou there, Lodowick? Give me ink and paper.

LODOWICK.

I will, my liege.

KING EDWARD.

And bid the Lords hold on their play at Chess,

For we will walk and meditate alone.

LODOWICK.

I will, my sovereign.

[Exit Lodowick.]

KING EDWARD.

This fellow is well read in poetry,

And hath a lusty and persuasive spirit;

I will acquaint him with my passion,

Which he shall shadow with a veil of lawn,

Through which the Queen of beauties Queen shall see

Her self the ground of my infirmity.

[Enter Lodowick.]

KING EDWARD. hast thou pen, ink, and paper ready, Lodowick?

LODOWICK.

Ready, my liege.

KING EDWARD.

Then in the summer arbor sit by me,

Make it our counsel house or cabinet:

Since green our thoughts, green be the conventicle,

Where we will ease us by disburdening them.

Now, Lodowick, invocate some golden Muse,

To bring thee hither an enchanted pen,

That may for sighs set down true sighs indeed,

Talking of grief, to make thee ready groan;

And when thou writest of tears, encouch the word

Before and after with such sweet laments,

That it may raise drops in a Tartar's eye,

And make a flintheart Scythian pitiful;

For so much moving hath a Poet's pen:

Then, if thou be a Poet, move thou so,

And be enriched by thy sovereign's love.

For, if the touch of sweet concordant strings

Could force attendance in the ears of hell,

How much more shall the strains of poets' wit

Beguile and ravish soft and humane minds?

LODOWICK.

To whom, my Lord, shall I direct my stile?

KING EDWARD.

To one that shames the fair and sots the wise;

Whose bod is an abstract or a brief,

Contains each general virtue in the world.

Better than beautiful thou must begin,

Devise for fair a fairer word than fair,

And every ornament that thou wouldest praise,

Fly it a pitch above the soar of praise.

For flattery fear thou not to be convicted;

For, were thy admiration ten times more,

Ten times ten thousand more the worth exceeds

Of that thou art to praise, thy praises worth.

Begin; I will to contemplate the while:

Forget not to set down, how passionate,

How heart sick, and how full of languishment,

Her beauty makes me.

LODOWICK.

Write I to a woman?

KING EDWARD.

What beauty else could triumph over me,

Or who but women do our love lays greet?

What, thinkest thou I did bid thee praise a horse?

LODOWICK.

Of what condition or estate she is,

Twere requisite that I should know, my Lord.

KING EDWARD.

Of such estate, that hers is as a throne,

And my estate the footstool where she treads:

Then maist thou judge what her condition is

By the proportion of her mightiness.

Write on, while I peruse her in my thoughts.—

Her voice to music or the nightingale—

To music every summer leaping swain

Compares his sunburnt lover when she speaks;

And why should I speak of the nightingale?

The nightingale sings of adulterate wrong,

And that, compared, is too satyrical;

For sin, though sin, would not be so esteemed,

But, rather, virtue sin, sin virtue deemed.

Her hair, far softer than the silk worm's twist,

Like to a flattering glass, doth make more fair

The yellow Amber:—like a flattering glass

Comes in too soon; for, writing of her eyes,

I'll say that like a glass they catch the sun,

And thence the hot reflection doth rebound

Against the breast, and burns my heart within.

Ah, what a world of descant makes my soul

Upon this voluntary ground of love!—

Come, Lodowick, hast thou turned thy ink to gold?

If not, write but in letters Capital

My mistress' name, and it will gild thy paper:

Read, Lord, read;

Fill thou the empty hollows of mine ears

With the sweet hearing of thy poetry.

LODOWICK.

I have not to a period brought her praise.

KING EDWARD.

Her praise is as my love, both infinite,

Which apprehend such violent extremes,

That they disdain an ending period.

Her beauty hath no match but my affection;

Hers more than most, mine most and more than more:

Hers more to praise than tell the sea by drops,

Nay, more than drop the massy earth by sands,

And sand by sand print them in memory:

Then wherefore talkest thou of a period

To that which craves unended admiration?

Read, let us hear.

LODOWICK.

'More fair and chaste than is the queen of shades,'—

KING EDWARD.

That line hath two faults, gross and palpable:

Comparest thou her to the pale queen of night,

Who, being set in dark, seems therefore light?

What is she, when the sun lifts up his head,

But like a fading taper, dim and dead?

My love shall brave the eye of heaven at noon,

And, being unmasked, outshine the golden sun.

LODOWICK.

What is the other fault, my sovereign Lord?

KING EDWARD.

Read o'er the line again.

LODOWICK.

'More fair and chaste'—

KING EDWARD.

I did not bid thee talk of chastity,

To ransack so the treasure of her mind;

For I had rather have her chased than chaste.

Out with the moon line, I will none of it;

And let me have her likened to the sun:

Say she hath thrice more splendour than the sun,

That her perfections emulate the sun,

That she breeds sweets as plenteous as the sun,

That she doth thaw cold winter like the sun,

That she doth cheer fresh summer like the sun,

The she doth dazzle gazers like the sun;

And, in this application to the sun,

Bid her be free and general as the sun,

Who smiles upon the basest weed that grows

As lovingly as on the fragrant rose.

Let's see what follows that same moonlight line.

LODOWICK.

'More fair and chaste than is the queen of shades,

More bold in constance'—

KING EDWARD.

In constance! than who?

LODOWICK.

'Than Judith was.'

KING EDWARD.

O monstrous line! Put in the next a sword,

And I shall woo her to cut of my head.

Blot, blot, good Lodowick! Let us hear the next.

LODOWICK.

There's all that yet is done.

KING EDWARD.

I thank thee then; thou hast done little ill,

But what is done, is passing, passing ill.

No, let the Captain talk of boisterous war,

The prisoner of emured dark constraint,

The sick man best sets down the pangs of death,

The man that starves the sweetness of a feast,

The frozen soul the benefit of fire,

And every grief his happy opposite:

Love cannot sound well but in lover's tongues;

Give me the pen and paper, I will write.

[Enter Countess.]

But soft, here comes the treasurer of my spirit.—

Lodowick, thou knowst not how to draw a battle;

These wings, these flankers, and these squadrons

Argue in thee defective discipline:

Thou shouldest have placed this here, this other here.

COUNTESS.

Pardon my boldness, my thrice gracious Lords;

Let my intrusion here be called my duty,

That comes to see my sovereign how he fares.

KING EDWARD.

Go, draw the same, I tell thee in what form.

LODOWICK.

I go.

[Exit Lodowick.]

COUNTESS.

Sorry I am to see my liege so sad:

What may thy subject do to drive from thee

Thy gloomy consort, sullome melancholy?

KING EDWARD.

Ah, Lady, I am blunt and cannot straw

The flowers of solace in a ground of shame:—

Since I came hither, Countess, I am wronged.

COUNTESS.

Now God forbid that any in my house

Should think my sovereign wrong! Thrice gentle King,

Acquaint me with your cause of discontent.

KING EDWARD.

How near then shall I be to remedy?

COUNTESS.

As near, my Liege, as all my woman's power

Can pawn it self to buy thy remedy.

KING EDWARD.

If thou speakst true, then have I my redress:

Engage thy power to redeem my Joys,

And I am joyful, Countess; else I die.

COUNTESS.

I will, my Liege.

KING EDWARD.

Swear, Countess, that thou wilt.

COUNTESS.

By heaven, I will.

KING EDWARD.

Then take thy self a little way a side,

And tell thy self, a King doth dote on thee;

Say that within thy power it doth lie

To make him happy, and that thou hast sworn

To give him all the Joy within thy power:

Do this, and tell me when I shall be happy.

COUNTESS.

All this is done, my thrice dread sovereign:

That power of love, that I have power to give,

Thou hast with all devout obedience;

Employ me how thou wilt in proof thereof.

KING EDWARD.

Thou hearst me say that I do dote on thee.

COUNTESS.

If on my beauty, take it if thou canst;

Though little, I do prize it ten times less;

If on my virtue, take it if thou canst,

For virtue's store by giving doth augment;

Be it on what it will, that I can give

And thou canst take away, inherit it.

KING EDWARD.

It is thy beauty that I would enjoy.

COUNTESS.

O, were it painted, I would wipe it off

And dispossess my self, to give it thee.

But, sovereign, it is soldered to my life:

Take one and both; for, like an humble shadow,

It haunts the sunshine of my summer's life.

KING EDWARD.

But thou maist lend it me to sport with all.

COUNTESS.

As easy may my intellectual soul

Be lent away, and yet my body live,

As lend my body, palace to my soul,

Away from her, and yet retain my soul.

My body is her bower, her Court, her abbey,

And she an Angel, pure, divine, unspotted:

If I should leave her house, my Lord, to thee,

I kill my poor soul and my poor soul me.

KING EDWARD.

Didst thou not swear to give me what I would?

COUNTESS.

I did, my liege, so what you would I could.

KING EDWARD.

I wish no more of thee than thou maist give:—

Nor beg I do not, but I rather buy—

That is, thy love; and for that love of thine

In rich exchange I tender to thee mine.

COUNTESS.

But that your lips were sacred, my Lord,

You would profane the holy name of love.

That love you offer me you cannot give,

For Caesar owes that tribute to his Queen;

That love you beg of me I cannot give,

For Sara owes that duty to her Lord.

He that doth clip or counterfeit your stamp

Shall die, my Lord; and will your sacred self

Commit high treason against the King of heaven,

To stamp his Image in forbidden metal,

Forgetting your allegiance and your oath?

In violating marriage sacred law,

You break a greater honor than your self:

To be a King is of a younger house

Than to be married; your progenitour,

Sole reigning Adam on the universe,

By God was honored for a married man,

But not by him anointed for a king.

It is a penalty to break your statutes,

Though not enacted with your highness' hand:

How much more, to infringe the holy act,

Made by the mouth of God, sealed with his hand?

I know, my sovereign, in my husband's love,

Who now doth loyal service in his wars,

Doth but so try the wife of Salisbury,

Whither she will hear a wanton's tale or no,

Lest being therein guilty by my stay,

>From that, not from my liege, I turn away.

                                                        [Exit.]

KING EDWARD.

Whether is her beauty by her words dying,

Or are her words sweet chaplains to her beauty?

Like as the wind doth beautify a sail,

And as a sail becomes the unseen wind,

So do her words her beauties, beauties words.

O, that I were a honey gathering bee,

To bear the comb of virtue from this flower,

And not a poison sucking envious spider,

To turn the juice I take to deadly venom!

Religion is austere and beauty gentle;

Too strict a guardian for so fair a ward!

O, that she were, as is the air, to me!

Why, so she is, for when I would embrace her,

This do I, and catch nothing but my self.

I must enjoy her; for I cannot beat

With reason and reproof fond love a way.

[Enter Warwick.]

Here comes her father: I will work with him,

To bear my colours in this field of love.

WARWICK.

How is it that my sovereign is so sad?

May I with pardon know your highness grief;

And that my old endeavor will remove it,

It shall not cumber long your majesty.

KING EDWARD.

A kind and voluntary gift thou proferest,

That I was forward to have begged of thee.

But, O thou world, great nurse of flattery,

Why dost thou tip men's tongues with golden words,

And peise their deeds with weight of heavy lead,

That fair performance cannot follow promise?

O, that a man might hold the heart's close book

And choke the lavish tongue, when it doth utter

The breath of falsehood not charactered there!

WARWICK.

Far be it from the honor of my age,

That I should owe bright gold and render lead;

Age is a cynic, not a flatterer.

I say again, that if I knew your grief,

And that by me it may be lessened,

My proper harm should buy your highness good.

KING EDWARD.

These are the vulgar tenders of false men,

That never pay the duty of their words.

Thou wilt not stick to swear what thou hast said;

But, when thou knowest my grief's condition,

This rash disgorged vomit of thy word

Thou wilt eat up again, and leave me helpless.

WARWICK.

By heaven, I will not, though your majesty

Did bid me run upon your sword and die.

KING EDWARD.

Say that my grief is no way medicinable

But by the loss and bruising of thine honour.

WARWICK.

If nothing but that loss may vantage you,

I would accompt that loss my vantage too.

KING EDWARD.

Thinkst that thou canst unswear thy oath again?

WARWICK.

I cannot; nor I would not, if I could.

KING EDWARD.

But, if thou dost, what shall I say to thee?

WARWICK.

What may be said to any perjured villain,

That breaks the sacred warrant of an oath.

KING EDWARD.

What wilt thou say to one that breaks an oath?

WARWICK.

That he hath broke his faith with God and man,

And from them both stands excommunicate.

KING EDWARD.

What office were it, to suggest a man

To break a lawful and religious vow?

WARWICK.

An office for the devil, not for man.

KING EDWARD.

That devil's office must thou do for me,

Or break thy oath, or cancel all the bonds

Of love and duty twixt thy self and me;

And therefore, Warwick, if thou art thy self,

The Lord and master of thy word and oath,

Go to thy daughter; and in my behalf

Command her, woo her, win her any ways,

To be my mistress and my secret love.

I will not stand to hear thee make reply:

Thy oath break hers, or let thy sovereign die.

[Exit.]

WARWICK.

O doting King! O detestable office!

Well may I tempt my self to wrong my self,

When he hath sworn me by the name of God

To break a vow made by the name of God.

What, if I swear by this right hand of mine

To cut this right hand off? The better way

Were to profane the Idol than confound it:

But neither will I do; I'll keep mine oath,

And to my daughter make a recantation

Of all the virtue I have preacht to her:

I'll say, she must forget her husband Salisbury,

If she remember to embrace the king;

I'll say, an oath may easily be broken,

But not so easily pardoned, being broken;

I'll say, it is true charity to love,

But not true love to be so charitable;

I'll say, his greatness may bear out the shame,

But not his kingdom can buy out the sin;

I'll say, it is my duty to persuade,

But not her honesty to give consent.

[Enter Countess.]

See where she comes; was never father had

Against his child an embassage so bad?

COUNTESS.

My Lord and father, I have sought for you:

My mother and the Peers importune you

To keep in presence of his majesty,

And do your best to make his highness merry.

WARWICK.

[Aside.] How shall I enter in this graceless arrant?

I must not call her child, for where's the father

That will in such a suit seduce his child?

Then, 'wife of Salisbury'; shall I so begin?

No, he's my friend, and where is found the friend

That will do friendship such indammagement?

[To the Countess.]

Neither my daughter nor my dear friend's wife,

I am not Warwick, as thou thinkst I am,

But an attorney from the Court of hell,

That thus have housed my spirit in his form,

To do a message to thee from the king.

The mighty king of England dotes on thee:

He that hath power to take away thy life,

Hath power to take thy honor; then consent

To pawn thine honor rather than thy life:

Honor is often lost and got again,

But life, once gone, hath no recovery.

The Sun, that withers hay, doth nourish grass;

The king, that would disdain thee, will advance thee.

The Poets write that great Achilles' spear

Could heal the wound it made: the moral is,

What mighty men misdo, they can amend.

The Lyon doth become his bloody jaws,

And grace his forragement by being mild,

When vassel fear lies trembling at his feet.

The king will in his glory hide thy shame;

And those that gaze on him to find out thee,

Will lose their eye-sight, looking in the Sun.

What can one drop of poison harm the Sea,

Whose huge vastures can digest the ill

And make it loose his operation?

The king's great name will temper thy misdeeds,

And give the bitter potion of reproach,

A sugared, sweet and most delicious taste.

Besides, it is no harm to do the thing

Which without shame could not be left undone.

Thus have I in his majesty's behalf

Appareled sin in virtuous sentences,

And dwell upon thy answer in his suit.

COUNTESS.

Unnatural besiege! woe me unhappy,

To have escaped the danger of my foes,

And to be ten times worse injured by friends!

Hath he no means to stain my honest blood,

But to corrupt the author of my blood

To be his scandalous and vile solicitor?

No marvel though the branches be then infected,

When poison hath encompassed the root:

No marvel though the leprous infant die,

When the stern dame invenometh the Dug.

Why then, give sin a passport to offend,

And youth the dangerous reign of liberty:

Blot out the strict forbidding of the law,

And cancel every cannon that prescribes

A shame for shame or penance for offence.

No, let me die, if his too boistrous will

Will have it so, before I will consent

To be an actor in his graceless lust.

WARWICK.

Why, now thou speakst as I would have thee speak:

And mark how I unsay my words again.

An honorable grave is more esteemed

Than the polluted closet of a king:

The greater man, the greater is the thing,

Be it good or bad, that he shall undertake:

An unreputed mote, flying in the Sun,

Presents a greater substance than it is:

The freshest summer's day doth soonest taint

The loathed carrion that it seems to kiss:

Deep are the blows made with a mighty Axe:

That sin doth ten times aggravate it self,

That is committed in a holy place:

An evil deed, done by authority,

Is sin and subornation: Deck an Ape

In tissue, and the beauty of the robe

Adds but the greater scorn unto the beast.

A spatious field of reasons could I urge

Between his glory, daughter, and thy shame:

That poison shews worst in a golden cup;

Dark night seems darker by the lightning flash;

Lilies that fester smell far worse than weeds;

And every glory that inclines to sin,

The shame is treble by the opposite.

So leave I with my blessing in thy bosom,

Which then convert to a most heavy curse,

When thou convertest from honor's golden name

To the black faction of bed blotting shame.

COUNTESS.

I'll follow thee; and when my mind turns so,

My body sink my soul in endless woe!

[Exeunt.]

SCENE II. The Same. A Room in the Castle.

[Enter at one door Derby from France, At an other door Audley with a Drum.]

DERBY.

Thrice noble Audley, well encountered here!

How is it with our sovereign and his peers?

AUDLEY.

Tis full a fortnight, since I saw his highness

What time he sent me forth to muster men;

Which I accordingly have done, and bring them hither

In fair array before his majesty.

What news, my Lord of Derby, from the Emperor?

DERBY.

As good as we desire: the Emperor

Hath yielded to his highness friendly aid,

And makes our king lieutenant general

In all his lands and large dominions;

Then via for the spatious bounds of France!

AUDLEY.

What, doth his highness leap to hear these news?

DERBY.

I have not yet found time to open them;

The king is in his closet, malcontent;

For what, I know not, but he gave in charge,

Till after dinner none should interrupt him:

The Countess Salisbury and her father Warwick,

Artois and all look underneath the brows.

AUDLEY.

Undoubtedly, then, some thing is amiss.

[Trumpet within.]

DERBY.

The Trumpets sound, the king is now abroad.

[Enter the King.]

AUDLEY.

Here comes his highness.

DERBY.

Befall my sovereign all my sovereign's wish!

KING EDWARD.

Ah, that thou wert a Witch to make it so!

DERBY.

The Emperour greeteth you.

[Presenting Letters.]

KING EDWARD.

—Would it were the Countess!

DERBY.

And hath accorded to your highness suite.

KING EDWARD.

—Thou liest, she hath not; but I would she had.

AUDLEY.

All love and duty to my Lord the King!

KING EDWARD.

Well, all but one is none.—What news with you?

AUDLEY.

I have, my liege, levied those horse and foot

According to your charge, and brought them hither.

KING EDWARD.

Then let those foot trudge hence upon those horse

According to our discharge, and be gone.—

Darby, I'll look upon the Countess' mind anon.

DERBY.

The Countess' mind, my liege?

KING EDWARD.

I mean the Emperour:—leave me alone.

AUDLEY.

What is his mind?

DERBY.

Let's leave him to his humor.

[Exeunt.]

KING EDWARD.

Thus from the heart's aboundance speaks the tongue;

Countess for Emperour: and indeed, why not?

She is as imperator over me

And I to her

Am as a kneeling vassal, that observes

The pleasure or displeasure of her eye.

[Enter Lodowick.]

What says the more than Cleopatra's match

To Caesar now?

LODOWICK.

That yet, my liege, ere night

She will resolve your majesty.

[Drum within.]

KING EDWARD.

What drum is this that thunders forth this march,

To start the tender Cupid in my bosom?

Poor shipskin, how it brawls with him that beateth it!

Go, break the thundring parchment bottom out,

And I will teach it to conduct sweet lines

Unto the bosom of a heavenly Nymph;

For I will use it as my writing paper,

And so reduce him from a scolding drum

To be the herald and dear counsel bearer

Betwixt a goddess and a mighty king.

Go, bid the drummer learn to touch the Lute,

Or hang him in the braces of his drum,

For now we think it an uncivil thing,

To trouble heaven with such harsh resounds:

Away!

[Exit.]

The quarrel that I have requires no arms

But these of mine: and these shall meet my foe

In a deep march of penetrable groans;

My eyes shall be my arrows, and my sighs

Shall serve me as the vantage of the wind,

To whirl away my sweetest artillery.

Ah, but, alas, she wins the sun of me,

For that is she her self, and thence it comes

That Poets term the wanton warrior blind;

But love hath eyes as judgement to his steps,

Till too much loved glory dazzles them.—

[Enter Lodowick.]

How now?

LODOWICK.

My liege, the drum that stroke the lusty march,

Stands with Prince Edward, your thrice valiant son.

[Enter Prince Edward.]

KING EDWARD.

I see the boy; oh, how his mother's face,

Modeled in his, corrects my strayed desire,

And rates my heart, and chides my thievish eye,

Who, being rich enough in seeing her,

Yet seeks elsewhere: and basest theft is that

Which cannot cloak it self on poverty.—

Now, boy, what news?

PRINCE EDWARD.

I have assembled, my dear Lord and father,

The choicest buds of all our English blood

For our affairs in France; and here we come

To take direction from your majesty.

KING EDWARD.

Still do I see in him delineate

His mother's visage; those his eyes are hers,

Who, looking wistely on me, make me blush:

For faults against themselves give evidence;

Lust is fire, and men like lanthornes show

Light lust within them selves, even through them selves.

Away, loose silks of wavering vanity!

Shall the large limit of fair Brittain

By me be overthrown, and shall I not

Master this little mansion of my self?

Give me an Armor of eternal steel!

I go to conquer kings; and shall I not then

Subdue my self? and be my enemy's friend?

It must not be.—Come, boy, forward, advance!

Let's with our colours sweet the Air of France.

[Enter Lodowick.]

LODOWICK.

My liege, the Countess with a smiling cheer

Desires access unto your Majesty.

KING EDWARD.

Why, there it goes! That very smile of hers

Hath ransomed captive France, and set the King,

The Dauphin, and the Peers at liberty.—

Go, leave me, Ned, and revel with thy friends.

[Exit Prince Edward.]

Thy mother is but black, and thou, like her,

Dost put it in my mind how foul she is.—

Go, fetch the Countess hither in thy hand,

And let her chase away these winter clouds,

For she gives beauty both to heaven and earth.

[Exit Lodowick.]

The sin is more to hack and hew poor men,

Than to embrace in an unlawful bed

The register of all rarities

Since Letherne Adam till this youngest hour.

[Enter Countess escorted by Lodowick.]

Go, Lodowick, put thy hand into my purse,

Play, spend, give, riot, waste, do what thou wilt,

So thou wilt hence awhile and leave me here.

[Exit Lodowick.]

Now, my soul's playfellow, art thou come

To speak the more than heavenly word of yea

To my objection in thy beauteous love?

COUNTESS.

My father on his blessing hath commanded—

KING EDWARD.

That thou shalt yield to me?

COUNTESS.

Aye, dear my liege, your due.

KING EDWARD.

And that, my dearest love, can be no less

Than right for right and tender love for love.

COUNTESS.

Then wrong for wrong and endless hate for hate.—

But,—sith I see your majesty so bent,

That my unwillingness, my husband's love,

Your high estate, nor no respect respected

Can be my help, but that your mightiness

Will overbear and awe these dear regards—

I bind my discontent to my content,

And what I would not I'll compel I will,

Provided that your self remove those lets

That stand between your highness' love and mine.

KING EDWARD.

Name them, fair Countess, and, by heaven, I will.

COUNTESS.

It is their lives that stand between our love,

That I would have choked up, my sovereign.

KING EDWARD.

Whose lives, my Lady?

COUNTESS.

My thrice loving liege,

Your Queen and Salisbury, my wedded husband,

Who living have that title in our love,

That we cannot bestow but by their death.

KING EDWARD.

Thy opposition is beyond our Law.

COUNTESS.

So is your desire: if the law

Can hinder you to execute the one,

Let it forbid you to attempt the other.

I cannot think you love me as you say,

Unless you do make good what you have sworn.

KING EDWARD.

No more; thy husband and the Queen shall die.

Fairer thou art by far than Hero was,

Beardless Leander not so strong as I:

He swom an easy current for his love,

But I will through a Hellespont of blood,

To arrive at Cestus where my Hero lies.

COUNTESS.

Nay, you'll do more; you'll make the River to

With their heart bloods that keep our love asunder,

Of which my husband and your wife are twain.

KING EDWARD.

Thy beauty makes them guilty of their death

And gives in evidence that they shall die;

Upon which verdict I, their Judge, condemn them.

COUNTESS.

[Aside.] O perjured beauty, more corrupted Judge!

When to the great Star-chamber o'er our heads

The universal Sessions calls to count

This packing evil, we both shall tremble for it.

KING EDWARD.

What says my fair love? is she resolute?

COUNTESS.

Resolute to be dissolute; and, therefore, this:

Keep but thy word, great king, and I am thine.

Stand where thou dost, I'll part a little from thee,

And see how I will yield me to thy hands.

    [Turning suddenly upon him, and shewing two Daggers.]

Here by my side doth hang my wedding knifes:

Take thou the one, and with it kill thy Queen,

And learn by me to find her where she lies;

And with this other I'll dispatch my love,

Which now lies fast a sleep within my heart:

When they are gone, then I'll consent to love.

Stir not, lascivious king, to hinder me;

My resolution is more nimbler far,

Than thy prevention can be in my rescue,

And if thou stir, I strike; therefore, stand still,

And hear the choice that I will put thee to:

Either swear to leave thy most unholy suit

And never hence forth to solicit me;

Or else, by heaven, this sharp pointed knife

Shall stain thy earth with that which thou would stain,

My poor chaste blood. Swear, Edward, swear,

Or I will strike and die before thee here.

KING EDWARD.

Even by that power I swear, that gives me now

The power to be ashamed of my self,

I never mean to part my lips again

In any words that tends to such a suit.

Arise, true English Lady, whom our Isle

May better boast of than ever Roman might

Of her, whose ransacked treasury hath taskt

The vain endeavor of so many pens:

Arise, and be my fault thy honor's fame,

Which after ages shall enrich thee with.

I am awakened from this idle dream.—

Warwick, my Son, Darby, Artois, and Audley!

Brave warriors all, where are you all this while?

[Enter all.]

Warwick, I make thee Warden of the North:

Thou, Prince of Wales, and Audley, straight to Sea;

Scour to New-haven; some there stay for me:

My self, Artois, and Darby will through Flanders,

To greet our friends there and to crave their aide.

This night will scarce suffice a faithful lover;

For, ere the Sun shall gild the eastern sky,

We'll wake him with our Marshall harmony.

[Exeunt.]

ACT III.

SCENE I. Flanders. The French Camp.

[Enter King John of France, his two sons, Charles of Normandy, and Phillip, and the Duke of Lorrain.]

KING JOHN.

Here, till our Navy of a thousand sail

Have made a breakfast to our foe by Sea,

Let us encamp, to wait their happy speed.—

Lorraine, what readiness is Edward in?

How hast thou heard that he provided is

Of marshall furniture for this exploit?

LORRAINE.

To lay aside unnecessary soothing,

And not to spend the time in circumstance,

Tis bruited for a certainty, my Lord,

That he's exceeding strongly fortified;

His subjects flock as willingly to war,

As if unto a triumph they were led.

CHARLES.

England was wont to harbour malcontents,

Blood thirsty and seditious Catelynes,

Spend thrifts, and such as gape for nothing else

But changing and alteration of the state;

And is it possible

That they are now so loyal in them selves?

LORRAINE.

All but the Scot, who solemnly protests,

As heretofore I have informed his grace,

Never to sheath his Sword or take a truce.

KING JOHN.

Ah, that's the anchorage of some better hope!

But, on the other side, to think what friends

King Edward hath retained in Netherland,

Among those ever-bibbing Epicures,

Those frothy Dutch men, puft with double beer,

That drink and swill in every place they come,

Doth not a little aggravate mine ire;

Besides, we hear, the Emperor conjoins,

And stalls him in his own authority;

But, all the mightier that their number is,

The greater glory reaps the victory.

Some friends have we beside domestic power;

The stern Polonian, and the warlike Dane,

The king of Bohemia, and of Sicily,

Are all become confederates with us,

And, as I think, are marching hither apace.

[Drum within.]

But soft, I hear the music of their drums,

By which I guess that their approach is near.

[Enter the King of Bohemia, with Danes, and a Polonian Captain, with other soldiers, another way.]

KING OF BOHEMIA.

King John of France, as league and neighborhood

Requires, when friends are any way distrest,

I come to aide thee with my country's force.

POLONIAN CAPTAIN.

And from great Musco, fearful to the Turk,

And lofty Poland, nurse of hardy men,

I bring these servitors to fight for thee,

Who willingly will venture in thy cause.

KING JOHN.

Welcome, Bohemian king, and welcome all:

This your great kindness I will not forget.

Besides your plentiful rewards in Crowns,

That from our Treasury ye shall receive,

There comes a hare brained Nation, decked in pride,

The spoil of whom will be a treble gain.

And now my hope is full, my joy complete:

At Sea, we are as puissant as the force

Of Agamemnon in the Haven of Troy;

By land, with Zerxes we compare of strength,

Whose soldiers drank up rivers in their thirst;

Then Bayardlike, blind, overweaning Ned,

To reach at our imperial diadem

Is either to be swallowed of the waves,

Or hacked a pieces when thou comest ashore.

[Enter Mariner.]

MARINER.

Near to the coast I have descried, my Lord,

As I was buy in my watchful charge,

The proud Armado of king Edward's ships:

Which, at the first, far off when I did ken,

Seemed as it were a grove of withered pines;

But, drawing near, their glorious bright aspect,

Their streaming Ensigns, wrought of coloured silk,

Like to a meadow full of sundry flowers,

Adorns the naked bosom of the earth:

Majestical the order of their course,

Figuring the horned Circle of the Moon:

And on the top gallant of the Admiral

And likewise all the handmaids of his train

The Arms of England and of France unite

Are quartered equally by Heralds' art:

Thus, tightly carried with a merry gale,

They plough the Ocean hitherward amain.

KING JOHN.

Dare he already crop the Fleur de Luce?

I hope, the honey being gathered thence,

He, with the spider, afterward approached,

Shall suck forth deadly venom from the leaves.—

But where's our Navy? how are they prepared

To wing them selves against this flight of Ravens?

MARINER.

They, having knowledge, brought them by the scouts,

Did break from Anchor straight, and, puffed with rage,

No otherwise then were their sails with wind,

Made forth, as when the empty Eagle flies,

To satisfy his hungry griping maw.

KING JOHN.

There's for thy news. Return unto thy bark;

And if thou scape the bloody stroke of war

And do survive the conflict, come again,

And let us hear the manner of the fight.

[Exit Mariner.]

Mean space, my Lords, tis best we be dispersed

To several places, least they chance to land:

First you, my Lord, with your Bohemian Troops,

Shall pitch your battailes on the lower hand;

My eldest son, the Duke of Normandy,

Together with the aide of Muscovites,

Shall climb the higher ground another way;

Here in the middle cost, betwixt you both,

Phillip, my youngest boy, and I will lodge.

So, Lors, be gone, and look unto your charge:

You stand for France, an Empire fair and large.

                                                     [Exeunt.]

Now tell me, Phillip, what is thy concept,

Touching the challenge that the English make?

PHILLIP.

I say, my Lord, claim Edward what he can,

And bring he ne'er so plain a pedigree,

Tis you are in the possession of the Crown,

And that's the surest point of all the Law:

But, were it not, yet ere he should prevail,

I'll make a Conduit of my dearest blood,

Or chase those straggling upstarts home again.

KING JOHN.

Well said, young Phillip! Call for bread and Wine,

That we may cheer our stomachs with repast,

To look our foes more sternly in the face.

      [A Table and Provisions brought in. The battle hard a far off.]

Now is begun the heavy day at Sea:

Fight, Frenchmen, fight; be like the field of Bears,

When they defend their younglings in the Caves!

Stir, angry Nemesis, the happy helm,

That, with the sulphur battles of your rage,

The English Fleet may be dispersed and sunk.

                [Shot.]

PHILLIP.

O Father, how this echoing Cannon shot,

Like sweet harmony, digests my eats!

KING JOHN.

Now, boy, thou hearest what thundering terror tis,

To buckle for a kingdom's sovereignty:

The earth, with giddy trembling when it shakes,

Or when the exhalations of the air

Breaks in extremity of lightning flash,

Affrights not more than kings, when they dispose

To shew the rancor of their high swollen hearts.

              [Retreat.]

Retreat is sounded; one side hath the worse;

O, if it be the French, sweet fortune, turn;

And, in thy turning, change the forward winds,

That, with advantage of a favoring sky,

Our men may vanquish, and the other fly!

[Enter Mariner.]

My heart misgives:—say, mirror of pale death,

To whom belongs the honor of this day?

Relate, I pray thee, if thy breath will serve,

The sad discourse of this discomfiture.

MARINER.

I will, my Lord.

My gracious sovereign, France hath ta'en the foil,

And boasting Edward triumphs with success.

These Iron hearted Navies,

When last I was reporter to your grace,

Both full of angry spleen, of hope, and fear,

Hasting to meet each other in the face,

At last conjoined; and by their Admiral

Our Admiral encountered many shot:

By this, the other, that beheld these twain

Give earnest penny of a further wrack,

Like fiery Dragons took their haughty flight;

And, likewise meeting, from their smoky wombs

Sent many grim Ambassadors of death.

Then gan the day to turn to gloomy night,

And darkness did as well enclose the quick

As those that were but newly reft of life.

No leisure served for friends to bid farewell;

And, if it had, the hideous noise was such,

As each to other seemed deaf and dumb.

Purple the Sea, whose channel filled as fast

With streaming gore, that from the maimed fell,

As did her gushing moisture break into

The crannied cleftures of the through shot planks.

Here flew a head, dissevered from the trunk,

There mangled arms and legs were tossed aloft,

As when a whirl wind takes the Summer dust

And scatters it in middle of the air.

Then might ye see the reeling vessels split,

And tottering sink into the ruthless flood,

Until their lofty tops were seen no more.

All shifts were tried, both for defence and hurt:

And now the effect of valor and of force,

Of resolution and of cowardice,

We lively pictures; how the one for fame,

The other by compulsion laid about;

Much did the Nonpareille, that brave ship;

So did the black snake of Bullen, then which

A bonnier vessel never yet spread sail.

But all in vain; both Sun, the Wind and tide,

Revolted all unto our foe men's side,

That we perforce were fain to give them way,

And they are landed.—Thus my tale is done:

We have untimely lost, and they have won.

KING JOHN.

Then rests there nothing, but with present speed

To join our several forces all in one,

And bid them battle, ere they range too far.

Come, gentle Phillip, let us hence depart;

This soldier's words have pierced thy father's heart.

[Exeunt.]

SCENE II. Picardy. Fields near Cressi.

[Enter two French men; a woman and two little Children meet them, and other Citizens.]

ONE.

Well met, my masters: how now? what's the news?

And wherefore are ye laden thus with stuff?

What, is it quarter day that you remove,

And carry bag and baggage too?

TWO.

Quarter day? Aye, and quartering day, I fear:

Have ye not heard the news that flies abroad?

ONE.

What news?

THREE.

How the French Navy is destroyed at Sea,

And that the English Army is arrived.

ONE.

What then?

TWO.

What then, quoth you? why, ist not time to fly,

When envy and destruction is so nigh?

ONE.

Content thee, man; they are far enough from hence,

And will be met, I warrant ye, to their cost,

Before they break so far into the Realm.

TWO.

Aye, so the Grasshopper doth spend the time

In mirthful jollity, till Winter come;

And then too late he would redeem his time,

When frozen cold hath nipped his careless head.

He, that no sooner will provide a Cloak,

Then when he sees it doth begin to reign,

May, peradventure, for his negligence,

Be throughly washed, when he suspects it not.

We that have charge and such a train as this,

Must look in time to look for them and us,

Least, when we would, we cannot be relieved.

ONE.

Belike, you then despair of all success,

And think your Country will be subjugate.

THREE.

We cannot tell; tis good to fear the worst.

ONE.

Yet rather fight, then, like unnatural sons,

Forsake your loving parents in distress.

TWO.

Tush, they that have already taken arms

Are many fearful millions in respect

Of that small handful of our enemies;

But tis a rightful quarrel must prevail;

Edward is son unto our late king's sister,

When John Valois is three degrees removed.

WOMAN.

Besides, there goes a Prophesy abroad,

Published by one that was a Friar once,

Whose Oracles have many times proved true;

And now he says, the time will shortly come,

When as a Lyon, roused in the west,

Shall carry hence the fluerdeluce of France:

These, I can tell ye, and such like surmises

Strike many French men cold unto the heart.

[Enter a French man.]

FOUR.

Fly, country men and citizens of France!

Sweet flowering peace, the root of happy life,

Is quite abandoned and expulst the land;

In stead of whom ransacked constraining war

Sits like to Ravens upon your houses' tops;

Slaughter and mischief walk within your streets,

And, unrestrained, make havoc as they pass;

The form whereof even now my self beheld

Upon this fair mountain whence I came.

For so far of as I directed mine eyes,

I might perceive five Cities all on fire,

Corn fields and vineyards, burning like an oven;

And, as the reaking vapour in the wind

Turned but aside, I like wise might discern

The poor inhabitants, escaped the flame,

Fall numberless upon the soldiers' pikes.

Three ways these dreadful ministers of wrath

Do tread the measures of their tragic march:

Upon the right hand comes the conquering King,

Upon the left his hot unbridled son,

And in the midst our nation's glittering host,

All which, though distant yet, conspire in one,

To leave a desolation where they come.

Fly therefore, Citizens, if you be wise,

Seek out some habitation further off:

Here is you stay, your wives will be abused,

Your treasure shared before your weeping eyes;

Shelter you your selves, for now the storm doth rise.

Away, away; me thinks I hear their drums:—

Ah, wretched France, I greatly fear thy fall;

Thy glory shaketh like a tottering wall.

[Exeunt.]

SCENE III. The same. Drums.

[Enter King Edward, and the Earl of Darby, With Soldiers, and Gobin de Grey.]

KING EDWARD.

Where's the French man by whose cunning guide

We found the shallow of this River Somme,

And had directions how to pass the sea?

GOBIN.

Here, my good Lord.

KING EDWARD.

How art thou called? tell me thy name.

GOBIN.

Gobin de Graie, if please your excellence.

KING EDWARD.

Then, Gobin, for the service thou hast done,

We here enlarge and give thee liberty;

And, for recompense beside this good,

Thou shalt receive five hundred marks in gold.—

I know not how, we should have met our son,

Whom now in heart I wish I might behold.

[Enter Artois.]

ARTOIS.

Good news, my Lord; the prince is hard at hand,

And with him comes Lord Awdley and the rest,

Whom since our landing we could never meet.

[Enter Prince Edward, Lord Awdley, and Soldiers.]

KING EDWARD.

Welcome, fair Prince! How hast thou sped, my son,

Since thy arrival on the coast of France?

PRINCE EDWARD.

Successfully, I thank the gracious heavens:

Some of their strongest Cities we have won,

As Harflew, Lo, Crotay, and Carentigne,

And others wasted, leaving at our heels

A wide apparent field and beaten path

For solitariness to progress in:

Yet those that would submit we kindly pardoned,

But who in scorn refused our proffered peace,

Endured the penalty of sharp revenge.

KING EDWARD.

Ah, France, why shouldest thou be thus obstinate

Against the kind embracement of thy friends?

How gently had we thought to touch thy breast

And set our foot upon thy tender mould,

But that, in froward and disdainful pride,

Thou, like a skittish and untamed colt,

Dost start aside and strike us with thy heels!

But tell me, Ned, in all thy warlike course,

Hast thou not seen the usurping King of France?

PRINCE EDWARD.

Yes, my good Lord, and not two hours ago,

With full a hundred thousand fighting men—

Upon the one side of the river's bank

And on the other both, his multitudes.

I feared he would have cropped our smaller power:

But happily, perceiving your approach,

He hath with drawn himself to Cressey plains;

Where, as it seemeth by his good array,

He means to bid us battle presently.

KING EDWARD.

He shall be welcome; that's the thing we crave.

[Enter King John, Dukes of Normandy and Lorrain, King of Boheme, young Phillip, and Soldiers.]

KING JOHN.

Edward, know that John, the true king of France,

Musing thou shouldst encroach upon his land,

And in thy tyranous proceeding slay

His faithful subjects and subvert his Towns,

Spits in thy face; and in this manner following

Obraids thee with thine arrogant intrusion:

First, I condemn thee for a fugitive,

A thievish pirate, and a needy mate,

One that hath either no abiding place,

Or else, inhabiting some barren soil,

Where neither herb or fruitful grain is had,

Doest altogether live by pilfering:

Next, insomuch thou hast infringed thy faith,

Broke leage and solemn covenant made with me,

I hold thee for a false pernicious wretch:

And, last of all, although I scorn to cope

With one so much inferior to my self,

Yet, in respect thy thirst is all for gold,

Thy labour rather to be feared than loved,

To satisfy thy lust in either part,

Here am I come, and with me have I brought

Exceeding store of treasure, pearl, and coin.

Leave, therefore, now to persecute the weak,

And armed entering conflict with the armed,

Let it be seen, mongest other petty thefts,

How thou canst win this pillage manfully.

KING EDWARD.

If gall or wormwood have a pleasant taste,

Then is thy salutation honey sweet;

But as the one hath no such property,

So is the other most satirical.

Yet wot how I regard thy worthless taunts:

If thou have uttered them to foil my fame

Or dim the reputation of my birth,

Know that thy wolvish barking cannot hurt;

If slyly to insinuate with the world,

And with a strumpet's artificial line

To paint thy vicious and deformed cause,

Be well assured, the counterfeit will fade,

And in the end thy foul defects be seen;

But if thou didst it to provoke me on,

As who should say I were but timorous.

Or, coldly negligent, did need a spur,

Bethink thy self how slack I was at sea,

How since my landing I have won no towns,

Entered no further but upon the coast,

And there have ever since securely slept.

But if I have been other wise employed,

Imagine, Valois, whether I intend

To skirmish, not for pillage, but for the Crown

Which thou dost wear; and that I vow to have,

Or one of us shall fall into his grave.

PRINCE EDWARD.

Look not for cross invectives at our hands,

Or railing execrations of despite:

Let creeping serpents, hid in hollow banks,

Sting with their tongues; we have remorseless swords,

And they shall plead for us and our affairs.

Yet thus much, briefly, by my father's leave:

As all the immodest poison of thy throat

Is scandalous and most notorious lies,

And our pretended quarrel is truly just,

So end the battle when we meet to day:

May either of us prosper and prevail,

Or, luckless, curst, receive eternal shame!

KING EDWARD.

That needs no further question; and I know,

His conscience witnesseth, it is my right.—

Therefore, Valois, say, wilt thou yet resign,

Before the sickles thrust into the Corn,

Or that inkindled fury turn to flame?

KING JOHN.

Edward, I know what right thou hast in France;

And ere I basely will resign my Crown,

This Champion field shall be a pool of blood,

And all our prospect as a slaughter house.

PRINCE EDWARD.

Aye, that approves thee, tyrant, what thou art:

No father, king, or shepherd of thy realm,

But one, that tears her entrails with thy hands,

And, like a thirsty tyger, suckst her blood.

AUDLEY.

You peers of France, why do you follow him

That is so prodigal to spend your lives?

CHARLES.

Whom should they follow, aged impotent,

But he that is their true borne sovereign?

KING EDWARD.

Obraidst thou him, because within his face

Time hath ingraved deep characters of age?

Know, these grave scholars of experience,

Like stiff grown oaks, will stand immovable,

When whirl wind quickly turns up younger trees.

DARBY.

Was ever any of thy father's house

King but thyself, before this present time?

Edward's great linage, by the mother's side,

Five hundred years hath held the scepter up:

Judge then, conspiratours, by this descent,

Which is the true borne sovereign, this or that.

PHILIP.

Father, range your battles, prate no more;

These English fain would spend the time in words,

That, night approaching, they might escape unfought.

KING JOHN.

Lords and my loving Subjects, now's the time,

That your intended force must bide the touch.

Therefore, my friends, consider this in brief:

He that you fight for is your natural King;

He against whom you fight, a foreigner:

He that you fight for, rules in clemency,

And reins you with a mild and gentle bit;

He against whom you fight, if he prevail,

Will straight inthrone himself in tyranny,

Makes slaves of you, and with a heavy hand

Curtail and curb your sweetest liberty.

Then, to protect your Country and your King,

Let but the haughty Courage of your hearts

Answer the number of your able hands,

And we shall quickly chase these fugitives.

For what's this Edward but a belly god,

A tender and lascivious wantoness,

That thother day was almost dead for love?

And what, I pray you, is his goodly guard?

Such as, but scant them of their chines of beef

And take away their downy featherbeds,

And presently they are as resty stiff,

As twere a many over ridden jades.

Then, French men, scorn that such should be your Lords,

And rather bind ye them in captive bands.

ALL FRENCHMEN.

Vive le Roy! God save King John of France!

KING JOHN.

Now on this plain of Cressy spread your selves,—

And, Edward, when thou darest, begin the fight.

    [Exeunt King John, Charles, Philip, Lorrain, Boheme, and Forces.]

KING EDWARD.

We presently will meet thee, John of France:—

And, English Lords, let us resolve this day,

Either to clear us of that scandalous crime,

Or be intombed in our innocence.

And, Ned, because this battle is the first

That ever yet thou foughtest in pitched field,

As ancient custom is of Martialists,

To dub thee with the tip of chivalry,

In solemn manner we will give thee arms.

Come, therefore, Heralds, orderly bring forth

A strong attirement for the prince my son.

[Enter four Heralds, bringing in a coat armour, a helmet, a lance, and a shield.]

KING EDWARD.

Edward Plantagenet, in the name of God,

As with this armour I impale thy breast,

So be thy noble unrelenting heart

Walled in with flint of matchless fortitude,

That never base affections enter there:

Fight and be valiant, conquer where thou comest!

Now follow, Lords, and do him honor to.

DARBY.

Edward Plantagenet, prince of Wales,

As I do set this helmet on thy head,

Wherewith the chamber of thy brain is fenst,

So may thy temples, with Bellona's hand,

Be still adorned with laurel victory:

Fight and be valiant, conquer where thou comest!

AUDLEY.

Edward Plantagenet, prince of Wales,

Receive this lance into thy manly hand;

Use it in fashion of a brazen pen,

To draw forth bloody stratagems in France,

And print thy valiant deeds in honor's book:

Fight and be valiant, vanquish where thou comest!

ARTOIS.

Edward Plantagenet, prince of Wales,

Hold, take this target, wear it on thy arm;

And may the view thereof, like Perseus' shield,

Astonish and transform thy gazing foes

To senseless images of meager death:

Fight and be valiant, conquer where thou comest!

KING EDWARD.

Now wants there nought but knighthood, which deferred

We leave, till thou hast won it in the field.

PRINCE EDWARD.

My gracious father and ye forward peers,

This honor you have done me, animates

And cheers my green, yet scarce appearing strength

With comfortable good presaging signs,

No other wise than did old Jacob's words,

When as he breathed his blessings on his sons.

These hallowed gifts of yours when I profane,

Or use them not to glory of my God,

To patronage the fatherless and poor,

Or for the benefit of England's peace,

Be numb my joints, wax feeble both mine arms,

Wither my heart, that, like a sapless tree,

I may remain the map of infamy.

KING EDWARD.

Then thus our steeled Battles shall be ranged:

The leading of the vaward, Ned, is thine;

To dignify whose lusty spirit the more,

We temper it with Audly's gravity,

That, courage and experience joined in one,

Your manage may be second unto none:

For the main battles, I will guide my self;

And, Darby, in the rearward march behind,

That orderly disposed and set in ray,

Let us to horse; and God grant us the day!

[Exeunt.]

SCENE IV. The Same.

[**Alarum. Enter a many French men flying. After them Prince Edward, running. Then enter King John and Duke of Lorrain.**]

KING JOHN.

Oh, Lorrain, say, what mean our men to fly?

Our number is far greater than our foes.

LORRAIN.

The garrison of Genoaes, my Lord,

That came from Paris weary with their march,

Grudging to be so suddenly imployd,

No sooner in the forefront took their place,

But, straight retiring, so dismayed the rest,

As likewise they betook themselves to flight,

In which, for haste to make a safe escape,

More in the clustering throng are pressed to death,

Than by the enemy, a thousand fold.

KING JOHN.

O hapless fortune! Let us yet assay,

If we can counsel some of them to stay.

[Exeunt.]

SCENE V. The Same.

[Enter King Edward and Audley.]

KING EDWARD.

Lord Audley, whiles our son is in the chase,

With draw our powers unto this little hill,

And here a season let us breath our selves.

AUDLEY.

I will, my Lord.

[Exit. Sound Retreat.]

KING EDWARD.

Just dooming heaven, whose secret providence

To our gross judgement is inscrutable,

How are we bound to praise thy wondrous works,

That hast this day given way unto the right,

And made the wicked stumble at them selves!

[Enter Artois.]

ARTOIS.

Rescue, king Edward! rescue for thy son!

KING EDWARD.

Rescue, Artois? what, is he prisoner,

Or by violence fell beside his horse?

ARTOIS.

Neither, my Lord: but narrowly beset

With turning Frenchmen, whom he did pursue,

As tis impossible that he should scape,

Except your highness presently descend.

KING EDWARD.

Tut, let him fight; we gave him arms to day,

And he is laboring for a knighthood, man.

[Enter Derby.]

DARBY.

The Prince, my Lord, the Prince! oh, succour him!

He's close incompast with a world of odds!

KING EDWARD.

Then will he win a world of honor too,

If he by valour can redeem him thence;

If not, what remedy? we have more sons

Than one, to comfort our declining age.

[Enter Audley.]

Renowned Edward, give me leave, I pray,

To lead my soldiers where I may relieve

Your Grace's son, in danger to be slain.

The snares of French, like Emmets on a bank,

Muster about him; whilest he, Lion like,

Intangled in the net of their assaults,

Franticly wrends, and bites the woven toil;

But all in vain, he cannot free him self.

KING EDWARD.

Audley, content; I will not have a man,

On pain of death, sent forth to succour him:

This is the day, ordained by destiny,

To season his courage with those grievous thoughts,

That, if he breaketh out, Nestor's years on earth

Will make him savor still of this exploit.

DARBY.

Ah, but he shall not live to see those days.

KING EDWARD.

Why, then his Epitaph is lasting praise.

AUDLEY.

Yet, good my Lord, tis too much willfulness,

To let his blood be spilt, that may be saved.

KING EDWARD.

Exclaim no more; for none of you can tell

Whether a borrowed aid will serve, or no;

Perhaps he is already slain or ta'en.

And dare a Falcon when she's in her flight,

And ever after she'll be haggard like:

Let Edward be delivered by our hands,

And still, in danger, he'll expect the like;

But if himself himself redeem from thence,

He will have vanquished cheerful death and fear,

And ever after dread their force no more

Than if they were but babes or Captive slaves.

AUDLEY.

O cruel Father! Farewell, Edward, then!

DARBY.

Farewell, sweet Prince, the hope of chivalry!

ARTOIS.

O, would my life might ransom him from death!

KING EDWARD.

But soft, me thinks I hear

[Retreat sounded.]

The dismal charge of Trumpets' loud retreat.

All are not slain, I hope, that went with him;

Some will return with tidings, good or bad.

[Enter Prince Edward in triumph, bearing in his hands his chivered Lance, and the King of Boheme, borne before, wrapped in the Colours. They run and imbrace him.]

AUDLEY.

O joyful sight! victorious Edward lives!

DERBY.

Welcome, brave Prince!

KING EDWARD.

Welcome, Plantagenet!

PRINCE EDWARD.

[Kneels and kisses his father's hand.]

First having done my duty as beseemed,

Lords, I regreet you all with hearty thanks.

And now, behold, after my winter's toil,

My painful voyage on the boisterous sea

Of wars devouring gulfs and steely rocks,

I bring my fraught unto the wished port,

My Summer's hope, my travels' sweet reward:

And here, with humble duty, I present

This sacrifice, this first fruit of my sword,

Cropped and cut down even at the gate of death,

The king of Boheme, father, whom I slew;

Whose thousands had entrenched me round about,

And lay as thick upon my battered crest,

As on an Anvil, with their ponderous glaves:

Yet marble courage still did underprop

And when my weary arms, with often blows,

Like the continual laboring Wood-man's Axe

That is enjoined to fell a load of Oaks,

Began to faulter, straight I would record

My gifts you gave me, and my zealous vow,

And then new courage made me fresh again,

That, in despite, I carved my passage forth,

And put the multitude to speedy flight.

Lo, thus hath Edward's hand filled your request,

And done, I hope, the duty of a Knight.

KING EDWARD.

Aye, well thou hast deserved a knighthood, Ned!

And, therefore, with thy sword, yet reaking warm

[His Sword borne by a Soldier.]

With blood of those that fought to be thy bane.

Arise, Prince Edward, trusty knight at arms:

This day thou hast confounded me with joy,

And proud thy self fit heir unto a king.

PRINCE EDWARD.

Here is a note, my gracious Lord, of those

That in this conflict of our foes were slain:

Eleven Princes of esteem, Four score Barons,

A hundred and twenty knights, and thirty thousand

Common soldiers; and, of our men, a thousand.

KING EDWARD.

Our God be praised! Now, John of France, I hope,

Thou knowest King Edward for no wantoness,

No love sick cockney, nor his soldiers jades.

But which way is the fearful king escaped?

PRINCE EDWARD.

Towards Poitiers, noble father, and his sons.

KING EDWARD.

Ned, thou and Audley shall pursue them still;

My self and Derby will to Calice straight,

And there be begirt that Haven town with siege.

Now lies it on an upshot; therefore strike,

And wistly follow, whiles the game's on foot.

What Picture's this?

PRINCE EDWARD.

A Pelican, my Lord,

Wounding her bosom with her crooked beak,

That so her nest of young ones may be fed

With drops of blood that issue from her heart;

The motto Sic & vos, 'and so should you'.

[Exeunt.]

ACT IV.

SCENE I. Bretagne. Camp of the English.

[Enter Lord Mountford with a Coronet in his hand; with him the Earl
of Salisbury.]

MOUNTFORD.

My Lord of Salisbury, since by your aide

Mine enemy Sir Charles of Blois is slain,

And I again am quietly possessed

In Brittain's Dukedom, know that I resolve,

For this kind furtherance of your king and you,

To swear allegiance to his majesty:

In sign whereof receive this Coronet,

Bear it unto him, and, withal, mine oath,

Never to be but Edward's faithful friend.

SALISBURY.

I take it, Mountfort. Thus, I hope, ere long

The whole Dominions of the Realm of France

Will be surrendered to his conquering hand.

[Exit Mountford.]

Now, if I knew but safely how to pass,

I would at Calice gladly meet his Grace,

Whether I am by letters certified

That he intends to have his host removed.

It shall be so, this policy will serve:—

Ho, whose within? Bring Villiers to me.

[Enter Villiers.]

Villiers, thou knowest, thou art my prisoner,

And that I might for ransom, if I would,

Require of thee a hundred thousand Francs,

Or else retain and keep thee captive still:

But so it is, that for a smaller charge

Thou maist be quit, and if thou wilt thy self.

And this it is: Procure me but a passport

Of Charles, the Duke of Normandy, that I

Without restraint may have recourse to Callis

Through all the Countries where he hath to do;

Which thou maist easily obtain, I think,

By reason I have often heard thee say,

He and thou were students once together:

And then thou shalt be set at liberty.

How saiest thou? wilt thou undertake to do it?

VILLIERS.

I will, my Lord; but I must speak with him.

SALISBURY.

Why, so thou shalt; take Horse, and post from hence:

Only before thou goest, swear by thy faith,

That, if thou canst not compass my desire,

Thou wilt return my prisoner back again;

And that shall be sufficient warrant for me.

VILLIERS.

To that condition I agree, my Lord,

And will unfainedly perform the same.

[Exit.]

SALISBURY.

Farewell, Villiers.—

Thus once i mean to try a French man's faith.

[Exit.]

SCENE II. Picardy. The English Camp before Calais.

[Enter King Edward and Derby, with Soldiers.]

KING EDWARD.

Since they refuse our proffered league, my Lord,

And will not ope their gates, and let us in,

We will intrench our selves on every side,

That neither vituals nor supply of men

May come to succour this accursed town:

Famine shall combat where our swords are stopped.

[Enter six poor Frenchmen.]

DERBY.

The promised aid, that made them stand aloof,

Is now retired and gone an other way:

It will repent them of their stubborn will.

But what are these poor ragged slaves, my Lord?

KING EDWARD.

Ask what they are; it seems, they come from Callis.

DERBY.

You wretched patterns of despair and woe,

What are you, living men or gliding ghosts,

Crept from your graves to walk upon the earth?

POOR.

No ghosts, my Lord, but men that breath a life

Far worse than is the quiet sleep of death:

We are distressed poor inhabitants,

That long have been diseased, sick, and lame;

And now, because we are not fit to serve,

The Captain of the town hath thrust us forth,

That so expense of victuals may be saved.

KING EDWARD.

A charitable deed, no doubt, and worthy praise!

But how do you imagine then to speed?

We are your enemies; in such a case

We can no less but put ye to the sword,

Since, when we proffered truce, it was refused.

POOR.

And if your grace no otherwise vouchsafe,

As welcome death is unto us as life.

KING EDWARD.

Poor silly men, much wronged and more distressed!

Go, Derby, go, and see they be relieved;

Command that victuals be appointed them,

And give to every one five Crowns a piece.

[Exeunt Derby and Frenchmen.]

The Lion scorns to touch the yielding prey,

And Edward's sword must flesh it self in such

As wilful stubbornness hath made perverse.

[Enter Lord Percy.]

KING EDWARD.

Lord Percy! welcome: what's the news in England?

PERCY.

The Queen, my Lord, comes here to your Grace,

And from her highness and the Lord viceregent

I bring this happy tidings of success:

David of Scotland, lately up in arms,

Thinking, belike, he soonest should prevail,

Your highness being absent from the Realm,

Is, by the fruitful service of your peers

And painful travel of the Queen her self,

That, big with child, was every day in arms,

Vanquished, subdued, and taken prisoner.

KING EDWARD.

Thanks, Percy, for thy news, with all my heart!

What was he took him prisoner in the field?

PERCY.

A Esquire, my Lord; John Copland is his name:

Who since, intreated by her Majesty,

Denies to make surrender of his prize

To any but unto your grace alone;

Whereat the Queen is grievously displeased.

KING EDWARD.

Well, then we'll have a Pursiuvant despatched,

To summon Copland hither out of hand,

And with him he shall bring his prisoner king.

PERCY.

The Queen's, my Lord, her self by this at Sea,

And purposeth, as soon as wind will serve,

To land at Callis, and to visit you.

KING EDWARD.

She shall be welcome; and, to wait her coming,

I'll pitch my tent near to the sandy shore.

[Enter a French Captain.]

CAPTAIN.

The Burgesses of Callis, mighty king,

Have by a counsel willingly decreed

To yield the town and Castle to your hands,

Upon condition it will please your grace

To grant them benefit of life and goods.

KING EDWARD.

They will so! Then, belike, they may command,

Dispose, elect, and govern as they list.

No, sirra, tell them, since they did refuse

Our princely clemency at first proclaimed,

They shall not have it now, although they would;

I will accept of nought but fire and sword,

Except, within these two days, six of them,

That are the wealthiest merchants in the town,

Come naked, all but for their linen shirts,

With each a halter hanged about his neck,

And prostrate yield themselves, upon their knees,

To be afflicted, hanged, or what I please;

And so you may inform their masterships.

[Exeunt Edward and Percy.]

CAPTAIN.

Why, this it is to trust a broken staff:

Had we not been persuaded, John our King

Would with his army have relieved the town,

We had not stood upon defiance so:

But now tis past that no man can recall,

And better some do go to wrack them all.

[Exit.]

SCENE III. Poitou. Fields near Poitiers. The French camp; Tent of the Duke of Normandy.

[Enter Charles of Normandy and Villiers.]

CHARLES.

I wonder, Villiers, thou shouldest importune me

For one that is our deadly enemy.

VILLIERS.

Not for his sake, my gracious Lord, so much

Am I become an earnest advocate,

As that thereby my ransom will be quit.

CHARLES.

Thy ransom, man? why needest thou talk of that?

Art thou not free? and are not all occasions,

That happen for advantage of our foes,

To be accepted of, and stood upon?

VILLIERS.

No, good my Lord, except the same be just;

For profit must with honor be comixt,

Or else our actions are but scandalous.

But, letting pass their intricate objections,

Wilt please your highness to subscribe, or no?

CHARLES.

Villiers, I will not, nor I cannot do it;

Salisbury shall not have his will so much,

To claim a passport how it pleaseth himself.

VILLIERS.

Why, then I know the extremity, my Lord;

I must return to prison whence I came.

CHARLES.

Return? I hope thou wilt not;

What bird that hath escaped the fowler's gin,

Will not beware how she's ensnared again?

Or, what is he, so senseless and secure,

That, having hardly past a dangerous gul,

Will put him self in peril there again?

VILLIERS.

Ah, but it is mine oath, my gracious Lord,

Which I in conscience may not violate,

Or else a kingdom should not draw me hence.

CHARLES.

Thine oath? why, tat doth bind thee to abide:

Hast thou not sworn obedience to thy Prince?

VILLIERS.

In all things that uprightly he commands:

But either to persuade or threaten me,

Not to perform the covenant of my word,

Is lawless, and I need not to obey.

CHARLES.

Why, is it lawful for a man to kill,

And not, to break a promise with his foe?

VILLIERS.

To kill, my Lord, when war is once proclaimed,

So that our quarrel be for wrongs received,

No doubt, is lawfully permitted us;

But in an oath we must be well advised,

How we do swear, and, when we once have sworn,

Not to infringe it, though we die therefore:

Therefore, my Lord, as willing I return,

As if I were to fly to paradise.

CHARLES.

Stay, my Villiers; thine honorable min

Deserves to be eternally admired.

Thy suit shall be no longer thus deferred:

Give me the paper, I'll subscribe to it;

And, wheretofore I loved thee as Villiers,

Hereafter I'll embrace thee as my self.

Stay, and be still in favour with thy Lord.

VILLIERS.

I humbly thank you grace; I must dispatch,

And send this passport first unto the Earl,

And then I will attend your highness pleasure.

CHARLES.

Do so, Villiers;—and Charles, when he hath need,

Be such his soldiers, howsoever he speed!

[Exit Villiers.]

[Enter King John.]

KING JOHN.

Come, Charles, and arm thee; Edward is entrapped,

The Prince of Wales is fallen into our hands,

And we have compassed him; he cannot escape.

CHARLES.

But will your highness fight to day?

KING JOHN.

What else, my son? he's scarce eight thousand strong,

And we are threescore thousand at the least.

CHARLES.

I have a prophecy, my gracious Lord,

Wherein is written what success is like

To happen us in this outrageous war;

It was delivered me at Cresses field

By one that is an aged Hermit there.

[Reads.] 'When feathered foul shall make thine army tremble,

And flint stones rise and break the battle ray,

Then think on him that doth not now dissemble;

For that shall be the hapless dreadful day:

Yet, in the end, thy foot thou shalt advance

As far in England as thy foe in France.'

KING JOHN.

By this it seems we shall be fortunate:

For as it is impossible that stones

Should ever rise and break the battle ray,

Or airy foul make men in arms to quake,

So is it like, we shall not be subdued:

Or say this might be true, yet in the end,

Since he doth promise we shall drive him hence

And forage their Country as they have done ours,

By this revenge that loss will seem the less.

But all are frivolous fancies, toys, and dreams:

Once we are sure we have ensnared the son,

Catch we the father after how we can.

[Exeunt.]

SCENE IV. The same. The English Camp.

[Enter Prince Edward, Audley, and others.]

PRINCE EDWARD.

Audley, the arms of death embrace us round,

And comfort have we none, save that to die

We pay sower earnest for a sweeter life.

At Cressey field out Clouds of Warlike smoke

Choked up those French mouths & dissevered them;

But now their multitudes of millions hide,

Masking as twere, the beauteous burning Sun,

Leaving no hope to us, but sullen dark

And eyeless terror of all ending night.

AUDLEY.

This sudden, mighty, and expedient head

That they have made, fair prince, is wonderful.

Before us in the valley lies the king,

Vantaged with all that heaven and earth can yield;

His party stronger battled than our whole:

His son, the braving Duke of Normandy,

Hath trimmed the Mountain on our right hand up

In shining plate, that now the aspiring hill

Shews like a silver quarry or an orb,

Aloft the which the Banners, bannarets,

And new replenished pendants cuff the air

And beat the winds, that for their gaudiness

Struggles to kiss them: on our left hand lies

Phillip, the younger issue of the king,

Coating the other hill in such array,

That all his guilded upright pikes do seem

Straight trees of gold, the pendants leaves;

And their device of Antique heraldry,

Quartered in colours, seeming sundry fruits,

Makes it the Orchard of the Hesperides:

Behind us too the hill doth bear his height,

For like a half Moon, opening but one way,

It rounds us in; there at our backs are lodged

The fatal Crossbows, and the battle there

Is governed by the rough Chattillion.

Then thus it stands: the valley for our flight

The king binds in; the hills on either hand

Are proudly royalized by his sons;

And on the Hill behind stands certain death

In pay and service with Chattillion.

PRINCE EDWARD.

Death's name is much more mighty than his deeds;

Thy parcelling this power hath made it more.

As many sands as these my hands can hold,

Are but my handful of so many sands;

Then, all the world, and call it but a power,

Easily ta'en up, and quickly thrown away:

But if I stand to count them sand by sand,

The number would confound my memory,

And make a thousand millions of a task,

Which briefly is no more, indeed, than one.

These quarters, squadrons, and these regiments,

Before, behind us, and on either hand,

Are but a power. When we name a man,

His hand, his foot, his head hath several strengths;

And being all but one self instant strength,

Why, all this many, Audley, is but one,

And we can call it all but one man's strength.

He that hath far to go, tells it by miles;

If he should tell the steps, it kills his heart:

The drops are infinite, that make a flood,

And yet, thou knowest, we call it but a Rain.

There is but one France, one king of France,

That France hath no more kings; and that same king

Hath but the puissant legion of one king,

And we have one: then apprehend no odds,

For one to one is fair equality.

[Enter an Herald from King John.]

PRINCE EDWARD.

What tidings, messenger? be plain and brief.

HERALD.

The king of France, my sovereign Lord and master,

Greets by me his foe, the Prince of Wales:

If thou call forth a hundred men of name,

Of Lords, Knights, Squires, and English gentlemen,

And with thy self and those kneel at his feet,

He straight will fold his bloody colours up,

And ransom shall redeem lives forfeited;

If not, this day shall drink more English blood,

Than ere was buried in our British earth.

What is the answer to his proffered mercy?

PRINCE EDWARD.

This heaven, that covers France, contains the mercy

That draws from me submissive orizons;

That such base breath should vanish from my lips,

To urge the plea of mercy to a man,

The Lord forbid! Return, and tell the king,

My tongue is made of steel, and it shall beg

My mercy on his coward burgonet;

Tell him, my colours are as red as his,

My men as bold, our English arms as strong:

Return him my defiance in his face.

HERALD.

I go.

[Exit.]

[Enter another Herald.]

PRINCE EDWARD.

What news with thee?

HERALD.

The Duke of Normandy, my Lord & master,

Pitying thy youth is so ingirt with peril,

By me hath sent a nimble jointed jennet,

As swift as ever yet thou didst bestride,

And therewithall he counsels thee to fly;

Else death himself hath sworn that thou shalt die.

PRINCE EDWARD.

Back with the beast unto the beast that sent him!

Tell him I cannot sit a coward's horse;

Bid him to day bestride the jade himself,

For I will stain my horse quite o'er with blood,

And double gild my spurs, but I will catch him;

So tell the carping boy, and get thee gone.

[Exit Herald.]

[Enter another Herald.]

HERALD.

Edward of Wales, Phillip, the second son

To the most mighty christian king of France,

Seeing thy body's living date expired,

All full of charity and christian love,

Commends this book, full fraught with prayers,

To thy fair hand and for thy hour of life

Intreats thee that thou meditate therein,

And arm thy soul for her long journey towards—

Thus have I done his bidding, and return.

PRINCE EDWARD.

Herald of Phillip, greet thy Lord from me:

All good that he can send, I can receive;

But thinkst thou not, the unadvised boy

Hath wronged himself in thus far tendering me?

Happily he cannot pray without the book—

I think him no divine extemporall—,

Then render back this common place of prayer,

To do himself good in adversity;

Beside he knows not my sins' quality,

And therefore knows no prayers for my avail;

Ere night his prayer may be to pray to God,

To put it in my heart to hear his prayer.

So tell the courtly wanton, and be gone.

HERALD.

I go.

[Exit.]

PRINCE EDWARD.

How confident their strength and number makes them!—

Now, Audley, sound those silver wings of thine,

And let those milk white messengers of time

Shew thy times learning in this dangerous time.

Thy self art bruis'd and bit with many broils,

And stratagems forepast with iron pens

Are texted in thine honorable face;

Thou art a married man in this distress,

But danger woos me as a blushing maid:

Teach me an answer to this perilous time.

AUDLEY.

To die is all as common as to live:

The one ince-wise, the other holds in chase;

For, from the instant we begin to live,

We do pursue and hunt the time to die:

First bud we, then we blow, and after seed,

Then, presently, we fall; and, as a shade

Follows the body, so we follow death.

If, then, we hunt for death, why do we fear it?

If we fear it, why do we follow it?

If we do fear, how can we shun it?

If we do fear, with fear we do but aide

The thing we fear to seize on us the sooner:

If we fear not, then no resolved proffer

Can overthrow the limit of our fate;

For, whether ripe or rotten, drop we shall,

As we do draw the lottery of our doom.

PRINCE EDWARD.

Ah, good old man, a thousand thousand armors

These words of thine have buckled on my back:

Ah, what an idiot hast thou made of life,

To seek the thing it fears! and how disgraced

The imperial victory of murdering death,

Since all the lives his conquering arrows strike

Seek him, and he not them, to shame his glory!

I will not give a penny for a life,

Nor half a halfpenny to shun grim death,

Since for to live is but to seek to die,

And dying but beginning of new life.

Let come the hour when he that rules it will!

To live or die I hold indifferent.

[Exeunt.]

SCENE V. The same. The French Camp.

[Enter King John and Charles.]

KING JOHN.

A sudden darkness hath defaced the sky,

The winds are crept into their caves for fear,

The leaves move not, the world is hushed and still,

The birds cease singing, and the wandering brooks

Murmur no wonted greeting to their shores;

Silence attends some wonder and expecteth

That heaven should pronounce some prophesy:

Where, or from whom, proceeds this silence, Charles?

CHARLES.

Our men, with open mouths and staring eyes,

Look on each other, as they did attend

Each other's words, and yet no creature speaks;

A tongue-tied fear hath made a midnight hour,

And speeches sleep through all the waking regions.

KING JOHN.

But now the pompous Sun, in all his pride,

Looked through his golden coach upon the world,

And, on a sudden, hath he hid himself,

That now the under earth is as a grave,

Dark, deadly, silent, and uncomfortable.

[A clamor of ravens.]

Hark, what a deadly outery do I hear?

CHARLES.

Here comes my brother Phillip.

KING JOHN.

All dismayed:

[Enter Phillip.]

What fearful words are those thy looks presage?

PHILLIP.

A flight, a flight!

KING JOHN.

Coward, what flight? thou liest, there needs no flight.

PHILLIP.

A flight.

KING JOHN.

Awake thy craven powers, and tell on

The substance of that very fear in deed,

Which is so ghastly printed in thy face:

What is the matter?

PHILLIP.

A flight of ugly ravens

Do croak and hover o'er our soldiers' heads,

And keep in triangles and cornered squares,

Right as our forces are embattled;

With their approach there came this sudden fog,

Which now hath hid the airy floor of heaven

And made at noon a night unnatural

Upon the quaking and dismayed world:

In brief, our soldiers have let fall their arms,

And stand like metamorphosed images,

Bloodless and pale, one gazing on another.

KING JOHN.

Aye, now I call to mind the prophesy,

But I must give no entrance to a fear.—

Return, and hearten up these yielding souls:

Tell them, the ravens, seeing them in arms,

So many fair against a famished few,

Come but to dine upon their handy work

And prey upon the carrion that they kill:

For when we see a horse laid down to die,

Although he be not dead, the ravenous birds

Sit watching the departure of his life;

Even so these ravens for the carcasses

Of those poor English, that are marked to die,

Hover about, and, if they cry to us,

Tis but for meat that we must kill for them.

Away, and comfort up my soldiers,

And sound the trumpets, and at once dispatch

This little business of a silly fraud.

[Exit Phillip.]

[Another noise. Salisbury brought in by a French Captain.]

CAPTAIN.

Behold, my liege, this knight and forty mo',

Of whom the better part are slain and fled,

With all endeavor sought to break our ranks,

And make their way to the encompassed prince:

Dispose of him as please your majesty.

KING JOHN.

Go, & the next bough, soldier, that thou seest,

Disgrace it with his body presently;

For I do hold a tree in France too good

To be the gallows of an English thief.

SALISBURY.

My Lord of Normandy, I have your pass

And warrant for my safety through this land.

CHARLES.

Villiers procured it for thee, did he not?

SALISBURY.

He did.

CHARLES.

And it is current; thou shalt freely pass.

KING JOHN.

Aye, freely to the gallows to be hanged,

Without denial or impediment.

Away with him!

CHARLES.

I hope your highness will not so disgrace me,

And dash the virtue of my seal at arms:

He hath my never broken name to shew,

Charactered with this princely hand of mine:

And rather let me leave to be a prince

Than break the stable verdict of a prince:

I do beseech you, let him pass in quiet.

KING JOHN.

Thou and thy word lie both in my command;

What canst thou promise that I cannot break?

Which of these twain is greater infamy,

To disobey thy father or thy self?

Thy word, nor no mans, may exceed his power;

Nor that same man doth never break his word,

That keeps it to the utmost of his power.

The breach of faith dwells in the soul's consent:

Which if thy self without consent do break,

Thou art not charged with the breach of faith.

Go, hang him: for thy license lies in me,

And my constraint stands the excuse for thee.

CHARLES.

What, am I not a soldier in my word?

Then, arms, adieu, and let them fight that list!

Shall I not give my girdle from my waste,

But with a gardion I shall be controlled,

To say I may not give my things away?

Upon my soul, had Edward, prince of Wales,

Engaged his word, writ down his noble hand

For all your knights to pass his father's land,

The royal king, to grace his warlike son,

Would not alone safe conduct give to them,

But with all bounty feasted them and theirs.

KING JOHN.

Dwelst thou on precedents? Then be it so!

Say, Englishman, of what degree thou art.

SALISBURY.

An Earl in England, though a prisoner here,

And those that know me, call me Salisbury.

KING JOHN.

Then, Salisbury, say whether thou art bound.

SALISBURY.

To Callice, where my liege, king Edward, is.

KING JOHN.

To Callice, Salisbury? Then, to Callice pack,

And bid the king prepare a noble grave,

To put his princely son, black Edward, in.

And as thou travelst westward from this place,

Some two leagues hence there is a lofty hill,

Whose top seems topless, for the embracing sky

Doth hide his high head in her azure bosom;

Upon whose tall top when thy foot attains,

Look back upon the humble vale beneath—

Humble of late, but now made proud with arms—

And thence behold the wretched prince of Wales,

Hooped with a bond of iron round about.

After which sight, to Callice spur amain,

And say, the prince was smothered and not slain:

And tell the king this is not all his ill;

For I will greet him, ere he thinks I will.

Away, be gone; the smoke but of our shot

Will choke our foes, though bullets hit them not.

[Exit.]

SCENE VI. The same. A Part of the Field of Battle.

[Alarum. Enter prince Edward and Artois.]

ARTOIS.

How fares your grace? are you not shot, my Lord?

PRINCE EDWARD.

No, dear Artois; but choked with dust and smoke,

And stepped aside for breath and fresher air.

ARTOIS.

Breath, then, and to it again: the amazed French

Are quite distract with gazing on the crows;

And, were our quivers full of shafts again,

Your grace should see a glorious day of this:—

O, for more arrows, Lord; that's our want.

PRINCE EDWARD.

Courage, Artois! a fig for feathered shafts,

When feathered fowls do bandy on our side!

What need we fight, and sweat, and keep a coil,

When railing crows outscold our adversaries?

Up, up, Artois! the ground it self is armed

With Fire containing flint; command our bows

To hurl away their pretty colored Ew,

And to it with stones: away, Artois, away!

My soul doth prophecy we win the day.

[Exeunt.]

SCENE VII. The same. Another Part of the Field of Battle.

[**Alarum. Enter King John.**]

KING JOHN.

Our multitudes are in themselves confounded,

Dismayed, and distraught; swift starting fear

Hath buzzed a cold dismay through all our army,

And every petty disadvantage prompts

The fear possessed abject soul to fly.

My self, whose spirit is steel to their dull lead,

What with recalling of the prophecy,

And that our native stones from English arms

Rebel against us, find myself attainted

With strong surprise of weak and yielding fear.

[**Enter Charles.**]

CHARLES.

Fly, father, fly! the French do kill the French,

Some that would stand let drive at some that fly;

Our drums strike nothing but discouragement,

Our trumpets sound dishonor and retire;

The spirit of fear, that feareth nought but death,

Cowardly works confusion on it self.

[**Enter Phillip.**]

PHILLIP.

Pluck out your eyes, and see not this day's shame!

An arm hath beat an army; one poor David

Hath with a stone foiled twenty stout Goliahs;

Some twenty naked starvelings with small flints,

Hath driven back a puissant host of men,

Arrayed and fenced in all accomplements.

KING JOHN.

Mordieu, they quait at us, and kill us up;

No less than forty thousand wicked elders

Have forty lean slaves this day stoned to death.

CHARLES.

O, that I were some other countryman!

This day hath set derision on the French,

And all the world will blurt and scorn at us.

KING JOHN.

What, is there no hope left?

PHILLIP.

No hope, but death, to bury up our shame.

KING JOHN.

Make up once more with me; the twentieth part

Of those that live, are men inow to quail

The feeble handful on the adverse part.

CHARLES.

Then charge again: if heaven be not opposed,

We cannot lose the day.

KING JOHN.

On, away!

[Exeunt.]

SCENE VIII. The same. Another Part of the Field of Battle.

[Enter Audley, wounded, & rescued by two squires.]

ESQUIRE.

How fares my Lord?

AUDLEY.

Even as a man may do,

That dines at such a bloody feast as this.

ESQUIRE.

I hope, my Lord, that is no mortal scar.

AUDLEY.

No matter, if it be; the count is cast,

And, in the worst, ends but a mortal man.

Good friends, convey me to the princely Edward,

That in the crimson bravery of my blood

I may become him with saluting him.

I'll smile, and tell him, that this open scar

Doth end the harvest of his Audley's war.

[Exeunt.]

SCENE IX. The same. The English Camp.

[Enter prince Edward, King John, Charles, and all, with Ensigns spread.]

PRINCE EDWARD.

Now, John in France, & lately John of France,

Thy bloody Ensigns are my captive colours;

And you, high vaunting Charles of Normandy,

That once to day sent me a horse to fly,

Are now the subjects of my clemency.

Fie, Lords, is it not a shame that English boys,

Whose early days are yet not worth a beard,

Should in the bosom of your kingdom thus,

One against twenty, beat you up together?

KING JOHN.

Thy fortune, not thy force, hath conquered us.

PRINCE EDWARD.

An argument that heaven aides the right.

[Enter Artois with Phillip.]

See, see, Artois doth bring with him along

The late good counsel giver to my soul.

Welcome, Artois; and welcome, Phillip, too:

Who now of you or I have need to pray?

Now is the proverb verified in you,

'Too bright a morning breeds a louring day.'

[Sound Trumpets. Enter Audley.]

But say, what grim discouragement comes here!

Alas, what thousand armed men of France

Have writ that note of death in Audley's face?

Speak, thou that wooest death with thy careless smile,

And lookst so merrily upon thy grave,

As if thou were enamored on thine end:

What hungry sword hath so bereaved thy face,

And lopped a true friend from my loving soul?

AUDLEY.

O Prince, thy sweet bemoaning speech to me

Is as a mournful knell to one dead sick.

PRINCE EDWARD.

Dear Audley, if my tongue ring out thy end,

My arms shall be thy grave: what may I do

To win thy life, or to revenge thy death?

If thou wilt drink the blood of captive kings,

Or that it were restorative, command

A Health of kings' blood, and I'll drink to thee;

If honor may dispense for thee with death,

The never dying honor of this day

Share wholly, Audley, to thy self, and live.

AUDLEY.

Victorious Prince,—that thou art so, behold

A Caesar's fame in king's captivity—

If I could hold him death but at a bay,

Till I did see my liege thy royal father,

My soul should yield this Castle of my flesh,

This mangled tribute, with all willingness,

To darkness, consummation, dust, and Worms.

PRINCE EDWARD.

Cheerily, bold man, thy soul is all too proud

To yield her City for one little breach;

Should be divorced from her earthly spouse

By the soft temper of a French man's sword?

Lo, to repair thy life, I give to thee

Three thousand Marks a year in English land.

AUDLEY.

I take thy gift, to pay the debts I owe:

These two poor Esquires redeemed me from the French

With lusty & dear hazard of their lives:

What thou hast given me, I give to them;

And, as thou lovest me, prince, lay thy consent

To this bequeath in my last testament.

PRINCE EDWARD.

Renowned Audley, live, and have from me

This gift twice doubled to these Esquires and thee:

But live or die, what thou hast given away

To these and theirs shall lasting freedom stay.

Come, gentlemen, I will see my friend bestowed

With in an easy Litter; then we'll march

Proudly toward Callis, with triumphant pace,

Unto my royal father, and there bring

The tribute of my wars, fair France his king.

[Exit.]

ACT V.

SCENE I. Picardy. The English Camp before Calais.

[Enter King Edward, Queen Phillip, Derby, soldiers.]

KING EDWARD.

No more, Queen Phillip, pacify your self;

Copland, except he can excuse his fault,

Shall find displeasure written in our looks.

And now unto this proud resisting town!

Soldiers, assault: I will no longer stay,

To be deluded by their false delays;

Put all to sword, and make the spoil your own.

[Enter six Citizens in their Shirts, bare foot, with halters about their necks.]

ALL.

Mercy, king Edward, mercy, gracious Lord!

KING EDWARD.

Contemptuous villains, call ye now for truce?

Mine ears are stopped against your bootless cries:—

Sound, drums alarum; draw threatening swords!

FIRST CITIZEN.

Ah, noble Prince, take pity on this town,

And hear us, mighty king:

We claim the promise that your highness made;

The two days' respite is not yet expired,

And we are come with willingness to bear

What torturing death or punishment you please,

So that the trembling multitude be saved.

KING EDWARD.

My promise? Well, I do confess as much:

But I do require the chiefest Citizens

And men of most account that should submit;

You, peradventure, are but servile grooms,

Or some felonious robbers on the Sea,

Whom, apprehended, law would execute,

Albeit severity lay dead in us:

No, no, ye cannot overreach us thus.

SECOND CITIZEN.

The Sun, dread Lord, that in the western fall

Beholds us now low brought through misery,

Did in the Orient purple of the morn

Salute our coming forth, when we were known;

Or may our portion be with damned fiends.

KING EDWARD.

If it be so, then let our covenant stand:

We take possession of the town in peace,

But, for your selves, look you for no remorse;

But, as imperial justice hath decreed,

Your bodies shall be dragged about these walls,

And after feel the stroke of quartering steel:

This is your doom;—go, soldiers, see it done.

QUEEN PHILLIP.

Ah, be more mild unto these yielding men!

It is a glorious thing to stablish peace,

And kings approach the nearest unto God

By giving life and safety unto men:

As thou intendest to be king of France,

So let her people live to call thee king;

For what the sword cuts down or fire hath spoiled,

Is held in reputation none of ours.

KING EDWARD.

Although experience teach us this is true,

That peaceful quietness brings most delight,

When most of all abuses are controlled;

Yet, insomuch it shall be known that we

As well can master our affections

As conquer other by the dint of sword,

Phillip, prevail; we yield to thy request:

These men shall live to boast of clemency,

And, tyranny, strike terror to thy self.

SECOND CITIZEN.

Long live your highness! happy be your reign!

KING EDWARD.

Go, get you hence, return unto the town,

And if this kindness hath deserved your love,

Learn then to reverence Edward as your king.—

[Exeunt Citizens.]

Now, might we hear of our affairs abroad,

We would, till gloomy Winter were o'er spent,

Dispose our men in garrison a while.

But who comes here?

[Enter Copland and King David.]

DERBY.

Copland, my Lord, and David, King of Scots.

KING EDWARD.

Is this the proud presumptuous Esquire of the North,

That would not yield his prisoner to my Queen?

COPLAND.

I am, my liege, a Northern Esquire indeed,

But neither proud nor insolent, I trust.

KING EDWARD.

What moved thee, then, to be so obstinate

To contradict our royal Queen's desire?

COPLAND.

No wilful disobedience, mighty Lord,

But my desert and public law at arms:

I took the king my self in single fight,

And, like a soldiers, would be loath to lose

The least pre-eminence that I had won.

And Copland straight upon your highness' charge

Is come to France, and with a lowly mind

Doth vale the bonnet of his victory:

Receive, dread Lord, the custom of my fraught,

The wealthy tribute of my laboring hands,

Which should long since have been surrendered up,

Had but your gracious self been there in place.

QUEEN PHILLIP.

But, Copland, thou didst scorn the king's command,

Neglecting our commission in his name.

COPLAND.

His name I reverence, but his person more;

His name shall keep me in allegiance still,

But to his person I will bend my knee.

KING EDWARD.

I pray thee, Phillip, let displeasure pass;

This man doth please me, and I like his words:

For what is he that will attempt great deeds,

And lose the glory that ensues the same?

All rivers have recourse unto the Sea,

And Copland's faith relation to his king.

Kneel, therefore, down: now rise, king Edward's knight;

And, to maintain thy state, I freely give

Five hundred marks a year to thee and thine.

[Enter Salisbury.]

Welcome, Lord Salisbury: what news from Brittain?

SALISBURY.

This, mighty king: the Country we have won,

And John de Mountford, regent of that place,

Presents your highness with this Coronet,

Protesting true allegiance to your Grace.

KING EDWARD.

We thank thee for thy service, valiant Earl;

Challenge our favour, for we owe it thee.

SALISBURY.

But now, my Lord, as this is joyful news,

So must my voice be tragical again,

And I must sing of doleful accidents.

KING EDWARD.

What, have our men the overthrow at Poitiers?

Or is our son beset with too much odds?

SALISBURY.

He was, my Lord: and as my worthless self

With forty other serviceable knights,

Under safe conduct of the Dauphin's seal,

Did travail that way, finding him distressed,

A troop of Lances met us on the way,

Surprised, and brought us prisoners to the king,

Who, proud of this, and eager of revenge,

Commanded straight to cut off all our heads:

And surely we had died, but that the Duke,

More full of honor than his angry sire,

Procured our quick deliverance from thence;

But, ere we went, 'Salute your king', quoth he,

'Bid him provide a funeral for his son:

To day our sword shall cut his thread of life;

And, sooner than he thinks, we'll be with him,

To quittance those displeasures he hath done.'

This said, we past, not daring to reply;

Our hearts were dead, our looks diffused and wan.

Wandering, at last we climed unto a hill,

>From whence, although our grief were much before,

Yet now to see the occasion with our eyes

Did thrice so much increase our heaviness:

For there, my Lord, oh, there we did descry

Down in a valley how both armies lay.

The French had cast their trenches like a ring,

And every Barricado's open front

Was thick embossed with brazen ordinance;

Here stood a battaile of ten thousand horse,

There twice as many pikes in quadrant wise,

Here Crossbows, and deadly wounding darts:

And in the midst, like to a slender point

Within the compass of the horizon,

As twere a rising bubble in the sea,

A Hasle wand amidst a wood of Pines,

Or as a bear fast chained unto a stake,

Stood famous Edward, still expecting when

Those dogs of France would fasten on his flesh.

Anon the death procuring knell begins:

Off go the Cannons, that with trembling noise

Did shake the very Mountain where they stood;

Then sound the Trumpets' clangor in the air,

The battles join: and, when we could no more

Discern the difference twixt the friend and foe,

So intricate the dark confusion was,

Away we turned our watery eyes with sighs,

As black as powder fuming into smoke.

And thus, I fear, unhappy have I told

The most untimely tale of Edward's fall.

QUEEN PHILLIP.

Ah me, is this my welcome into France?

Is this the comfort that I looked to have,

When I should meet with my beloved son?

Sweet Ned, I would thy mother in the sea

Had been prevented of this mortal grief!

KING EDWARD.

Content thee, Phillip; tis not tears will serve

To call him back, if he be taken hence:

Comfort thy self, as I do, gentle Queen,

With hope of sharp, unheard of, dire revenge.—

He bids me to provide his funeral,

And so I will; but all the Peers in France

Shall mourners be, and weep out bloody tears,

Until their empty veins be dry and sere:

The pillars of his hearse shall be his bones;

The mould that covers him, their City ashes;

His knell, the groaning cries of dying men;

And, in the stead of tapers on his tomb,

An hundred fifty towers shall burning blaze,

While we bewail our valiant son's decease.

[After a flourish, sounded within, enter an herald.]

HERALD.

Rejoice, my Lord; ascend the imperial throne!

The mighty and redoubted prince of Wales,

Great servitor to bloody Mars in arms,

The French man's terror, and his country's fame,

Triumphant rideth like a Roman peer,

And, lowly at his stirrup, comes afoot

King John of France, together with his son,

In captive bonds; whose diadem he brings

To crown thee with, and to proclaim thee king.

KING EDWARD.

Away with mourning, Phillip, wipe thine eyes;—

Sound, Trumpets, welcome in Plantagenet!

[Enter Prince Edward, king John, Phillip, Audley, Artois.]

As things long lost, when they are found again,

So doth my son rejoice his father's heart,

For whom even now my soul was much perplexed.

QUEEN PHILLIP.

Be this a token to express my joy,

[Kisses him.]

For inward passion will not let me speak.

PRINCE EDWARD.

My gracious father, here receive the gift.

[Presenting him with King John's crown.]

This wreath of conquest and reward of war,

Got with as mickle peril of our lives,

As ere was thing of price before this day;

Install your highness in your proper right:

And, herewithall, I render to your hands

These prisoners, chief occasion of our strife.

KING EDWARD.

So, John of France, I see you keep your word:

You promised to be sooner with our self

Than we did think for, and tis so in deed:

But, had you done at first as now you do,

How many civil towns had stood untouched,

That now are turned to ragged heaps of stones!

How many people's lives mightst thou have saved,

That are untimely sunk into their graves!

KING JOHN.

Edward, recount not things irrevocable;

Tell me what ransom thou requirest to have.

KING EDWARD.

Thy ransom, John, hereafter shall be known:

But first to England thou must cross the seas,

To see what entertainment it affords;

How ere it falls, it cannot be so bad,

As ours hath been since we arrived in France.

KING JOHN.

Accursed man! of this I was foretold,

But did misconster what the prophet told.

PRINCE EDWARD.

Now, father, this petition Edward makes

To thee, whose grace hath been his strongest shield,

That, as thy pleasure chose me for the man

To be the instrument to shew thy power,

So thou wilt grant that many princes more,

Bred and brought up within that little Isle,

May still be famous for like victories!

And, for my part, the bloody scars I bear,

And weary nights that I have watched in field,

The dangerous conflicts I have often had,

The fearful menaces were proffered me,

The heat and cold and what else might displease:

I wish were now redoubled twenty fold,

So that hereafter ages, when they read

The painful traffic of my tender youth,

Might thereby be inflamed with such resolve,

As not the territories of France alone,

But likewise Spain, Turkey, and what countries else

That justly would provoke fair England's ire,

Might, at their presence, tremble and retire.

KING EDWARD.

Here, English Lords, we do proclaim a rest,

An intercession of our painful arms:

Sheath up your swords, refresh your weary limbs,

Peruse your spoils; and, after we have breathed

A day or two within this haven town,

God willing, then for England we'll be shipped;

Where, in a happy hour, I trust, we shall

Arrive, three kings, two princes, and a queen.

FINISH

CYMBELINE, KING OF BRITAIN

Dramatis Personæ

CYMBELINE, King of Britain

CLOTEN, son to the Queen by a former husband

POSTHUMUS LEONATUS, a gentleman, husband to Imogen

BELARIUS, a banished lord, disguised under the name of Morgan

GUIDERIUS and ARVIRAGUS, sons to Cymbeline, disguised under the names of POLYDORE and CADWAL, supposed sons to Belarius

PHILARIO, Italian, friend to Posthumus

IACHIMO, Italian, friend to Philario

CAIUS LUCIUS, General of the Roman forces

PISANIO, servant to Posthumus

CORNELIUS, a physician

A SOOTHSAYER

A ROMAN CAPTAIN

TWO BRITISH CAPTAINS

A FRENCH GENTLEMAN, friend to Philario

TWO LORDS of Cymbeline's court

TWO GENTLEMEN of the same

TWO GAOLERS

QUEEN, wife to Cymbeline

IMOGEN, daughter to Cymbeline by a former queen

HELEN, a lady attending on Imogen

APPARITIONS

Lords, Ladies, Roman Senators, Tribunes, a Dutch Gentleman, a Spanish Gentleman, Musicians, Officers, Captains, Soldiers, Messengers, and Attendants

SCENE: Britain; Italy.

ACT I

SCENE I. Britain. The garden of Cymbeline's palace.

Enter two Gentlemen.

FIRST GENTLEMAN.

You do not meet a man but frowns; our bloods

No more obey the heavens than our courtiers

Still seem as does the King's.

SECOND GENTLEMAN.

But what's the matter?

FIRST GENTLEMAN.

His daughter, and the heir of's kingdom, whom

He purpos'd to his wife's sole son—a widow

That late he married—hath referr'd herself

Unto a poor but worthy gentleman. She's wedded;

Her husband banish'd; she imprison'd. All

Is outward sorrow, though I think the King

Be touch'd at very heart.

SECOND GENTLEMAN.

None but the King?

FIRST GENTLEMAN.

He that hath lost her too. So is the Queen,

That most desir'd the match. But not a courtier,

Although they wear their faces to the bent

Of the King's looks, hath a heart that is not

Glad at the thing they scowl at.

SECOND GENTLEMAN.

And why so?

FIRST GENTLEMAN.

He that hath miss'd the Princess is a thing

Too bad for bad report; and he that hath her—

I mean that married her, alack, good man!

And therefore banish'd—is a creature such

As, to seek through the regions of the earth

For one his like, there would be something failing

In him that should compare. I do not think

So fair an outward and such stuff within

Endows a man but he.

SECOND GENTLEMAN.

You speak him far.

FIRST GENTLEMAN.

I do extend him, sir, within himself;

Crush him together rather than unfold

His measure duly.

SECOND GENTLEMAN.

What's his name and birth?

FIRST GENTLEMAN.

I cannot delve him to the root; his father

Was call'd Sicilius, who did join his honour

Against the Romans with Cassibelan,

But had his titles by Tenantius, whom

He serv'd with glory and admir'd success,

So gain'd the sur-addition Leonatus;

And had, besides this gentleman in question,

Two other sons, who, in the wars o' th' time,

Died with their swords in hand; for which their father,

Then old and fond of issue, took such sorrow

That he quit being; and his gentle lady,

Big of this gentleman, our theme, deceas'd

As he was born. The King he takes the babe

To his protection, calls him Posthumus Leonatus,

Breeds him and makes him of his bed-chamber,

Puts to him all the learnings that his time

Could make him the receiver of; which he took,

As we do air, fast as 'twas minist'red,

And in's spring became a harvest, liv'd in court—

Which rare it is to do—most prais'd, most lov'd,

A sample to the youngest; to th' more mature

A glass that feated them; and to the graver

A child that guided dotards. To his mistress,

For whom he now is banish'd, her own price

Proclaims how she esteem'd him and his virtue;

By her election may be truly read

What kind of man he is.

SECOND GENTLEMAN.

I honour him

Even out of your report. But pray you tell me,

Is she sole child to th' King?

FIRST GENTLEMAN.

His only child.

He had two sons—if this be worth your hearing,

Mark it—the eldest of them at three years old,

I' th' swathing clothes the other, from their nursery

Were stol'n; and to this hour no guess in knowledge

Which way they went.

SECOND GENTLEMAN.

How long is this ago?

FIRST GENTLEMAN.

Some twenty years.

SECOND GENTLEMAN.

That a king's children should be so convey'd,

So slackly guarded, and the search so slow

That could not trace them!

FIRST GENTLEMAN.

Howsoe'er 'tis strange,

Or that the negligence may well be laugh'd at,

Yet is it true, sir.

SECOND GENTLEMAN.

I do well believe you.

FIRST GENTLEMAN.

We must forbear; here comes the gentleman,

The Queen, and Princess.

[Exeunt.]

SCENE II. The same.

Enter Queen, Posthumus and Imogen.

QUEEN.

No, be assur'd you shall not find me, daughter,

After the slander of most stepmothers,

Evil-ey'd unto you. You're my prisoner, but

Your gaoler shall deliver you the keys

That lock up your restraint. For you, Posthumus,

So soon as I can win th' offended King,

I will be known your advocate. Marry, yet

The fire of rage is in him, and 'twere good

You lean'd unto his sentence with what patience

Your wisdom may inform you.

POSTHUMUS.

Please your Highness,

I will from hence today.

QUEEN.

You know the peril.

I'll fetch a turn about the garden, pitying

The pangs of barr'd affections, though the King

Hath charg'd you should not speak together.

[Exit.]

IMOGEN.

O dissembling courtesy! How fine this tyrant

Can tickle where she wounds! My dearest husband,

I something fear my father's wrath, but nothing

(Always reserv'd my holy duty) what

His rage can do on me. You must be gone;

And I shall here abide the hourly shot

Of angry eyes, not comforted to live

But that there is this jewel in the world

That I may see again.

POSTHUMUS.

My queen! my mistress!

O lady, weep no more, lest I give cause

To be suspected of more tenderness

Than doth become a man. I will remain

The loyal'st husband that did e'er plight troth;

My residence in Rome at one Philario's,

Who to my father was a friend, to me

Known but by letter; thither write, my queen,

And with mine eyes I'll drink the words you send,

Though ink be made of gall.

Enter Queen.

QUEEN.

Be brief, I pray you.

If the King come, I shall incur I know not

How much of his displeasure. [Aside.] Yet I'll move him

To walk this way. I never do him wrong

But he does buy my injuries, to be friends;

Pays dear for my offences.

[Exit.]

POSTHUMUS.

Should we be taking leave

As long a term as yet we have to live,

The loathness to depart would grow. Adieu!

IMOGEN.

Nay, stay a little.

Were you but riding forth to air yourself,

Such parting were too petty. Look here, love:

This diamond was my mother's; take it, heart;

But keep it till you woo another wife,

When Imogen is dead.

POSTHUMUS.

How, how? Another?

You gentle gods, give me but this I have,

And sear up my embracements from a next

With bonds of death! Remain, remain thou here

[Puts on the ring.]

While sense can keep it on. And, sweetest, fairest,

As I my poor self did exchange for you,

To your so infinite loss, so in our trifles

I still win of you. For my sake wear this;

It is a manacle of love; I'll place it

Upon this fairest prisoner.

[Puts a bracelet on her arm.]

IMOGEN.

O the gods!

When shall we see again?

Enter Cymbeline and Lords.

POSTHUMUS.

Alack, the King!

CYMBELINE.

Thou basest thing, avoid; hence from my sight

If after this command thou fraught the court

With thy unworthiness, thou diest. Away!

Thou'rt poison to my blood.

POSTHUMUS.

The gods protect you,

And bless the good remainders of the court!

I am gone.

[Exit.]

IMOGEN.

There cannot be a pinch in death

More sharp than this is.

CYMBELINE.

O disloyal thing,

That shouldst repair my youth, thou heap'st

A year's age on me!

IMOGEN.

I beseech you, sir,

Harm not yourself with your vexation.

I am senseless of your wrath; a touch more rare

Subdues all pangs, all fears.

CYMBELINE.

Past grace? obedience?

IMOGEN.

Past hope, and in despair; that way past grace.

CYMBELINE.

That mightst have had the sole son of my queen!

IMOGEN.

O blessed that I might not! I chose an eagle,

And did avoid a puttock.

CYMBELINE.

Thou took'st a beggar, wouldst have made my throne

A seat for baseness.

IMOGEN.

No; I rather added

A lustre to it.

CYMBELINE.

O thou vile one!

IMOGEN.

Sir,

It is your fault that I have lov'd Posthumus.

You bred him as my playfellow, and he is

A man worth any woman; overbuys me

Almost the sum he pays.

CYMBELINE.

What, art thou mad?

IMOGEN.

Almost, sir. Heaven restore me! Would I were

A neat-herd's daughter, and my Leonatus

Our neighbour shepherd's son!

Enter Queen.

CYMBELINE.

Thou foolish thing!

[To the Queen.] They were again together. You have done

Not after our command. Away with her,

And pen her up.

QUEEN.

Beseech your patience. Peace,

Dear lady daughter, peace!—Sweet sovereign,

Leave us to ourselves, and make yourself some comfort

Out of your best advice.

CYMBELINE.

Nay, let her languish

A drop of blood a day and, being aged,

Die of this folly.

[Exit with Lords.]

Enter Pisanio.

QUEEN.

Fie! you must give way.

Here is your servant. How now, sir! What news?

PISANIO.

My lord your son drew on my master.

QUEEN.

Ha!

No harm, I trust, is done?

PISANIO.

There might have been,

But that my master rather play'd than fought,

And had no help of anger; they were parted

By gentlemen at hand.

QUEEN.

I am very glad on't.

IMOGEN.

Your son's my father's friend; he takes his part

To draw upon an exile! O brave sir!

I would they were in Afric both together;

Myself by with a needle, that I might prick

The goer-back. Why came you from your master?

PISANIO.

On his command. He would not suffer me

To bring him to the haven; left these notes

Of what commands I should be subject to,

When't pleas'd you to employ me.

QUEEN.

This hath been

Your faithful servant. I dare lay mine honour

He will remain so.

PISANIO.

I humbly thank your Highness.

QUEEN.

Pray walk awhile.

IMOGEN.

About some half-hour hence,

Pray you speak with me.

You shall at least go see my lord aboard.

For this time leave me.

[Exeunt.]

169

SCENE III. Britain. A public place.

Enter Cloten and two Lords.

FIRST LORD.

Sir, I would advise you to shift a shirt; the violence of action hath made you reek as a sacrifice. Where air comes out, air comes in; there's none abroad so wholesome as that you vent.

CLOTEN.

If my shirt were bloody, then to shift it. Have I hurt him?

SECOND LORD.

[Aside.] No, faith; not so much as his patience.

FIRST LORD.

Hurt him! His body's a passable carcass if he be not hurt. It is a throughfare for steel if it be not hurt.

SECOND LORD.

[Aside.] His steel was in debt; it went o' th' backside the town.

CLOTEN.

The villain would not stand me.

SECOND LORD.

[Aside.] No; but he fled forward still, toward your face.

FIRST LORD.

Stand you? You have land enough of your own; but he added to your having, gave you some ground.

SECOND LORD.

[Aside.] As many inches as you have oceans.

Puppies!

CLOTEN.

I would they had not come between us.

SECOND LORD.

[Aside.] So would I, till you had measur'd how long a fool you were upon the ground.

CLOTEN.

And that she should love this fellow, and refuse me!

SECOND LORD.

[Aside.] If it be a sin to make a true election, she is damn'd.

FIRST LORD.

Sir, as I told you always, her beauty and her brain go not together; she's a good sign, but I have seen small reflection of her wit.

SECOND LORD.

[Aside.] She shines not upon fools, lest the reflection should hurt her.

CLOTEN.

Come, I'll to my chamber. Would there had been some hurt done!

SECOND LORD.

[Aside.] I wish not so; unless it had been the fall of an ass, which is no great hurt.

CLOTEN.

You'll go with us?

FIRST LORD.

I'll attend your lordship.

CLOTEN.

Nay, come, let's go together.

SECOND LORD.

Well, my lord.

[Exeunt.]

<u>SCENE IV. Britain. Cymbeline's palace.</u>

Enter Imogen and Pisanio.

IMOGEN.

I would thou grew'st unto the shores o' th' haven,

And questioned'st every sail; if he should write,

And I not have it, 'twere a paper lost,

As offer'd mercy is. What was the last

That he spake to thee?

PISANIO.

It was: his queen, his queen!

IMOGEN.

Then wav'd his handkerchief?

PISANIO.

And kiss'd it, madam.

IMOGEN.

Senseless linen, happier therein than I!

And that was all?

PISANIO.

No, madam; for so long

As he could make me with his eye, or ear

Distinguish him from others, he did keep

The deck, with glove, or hat, or handkerchief,

Still waving, as the fits and stirs of's mind

Could best express how slow his soul sail'd on,

How swift his ship.

IMOGEN.

Thou shouldst have made him

As little as a crow, or less, ere left

To after-eye him.

PISANIO.

Madam, so I did.

IMOGEN.

I would have broke mine eyestrings, crack'd them but

To look upon him, till the diminution

Of space had pointed him sharp as my needle;

Nay, followed him till he had melted from

The smallness of a gnat to air, and then

Have turn'd mine eye and wept. But, good Pisanio,

When shall we hear from him?

PISANIO.

Be assur'd, madam,

With his next vantage.

IMOGEN.

I did not take my leave of him, but had

Most pretty things to say. Ere I could tell him

How I would think on him at certain hours

Such thoughts and such; or I could make him swear

The shes of Italy should not betray

Mine interest and his honour; or have charg'd him,

At the sixth hour of morn, at noon, at midnight,

T' encounter me with orisons, for then

I am in heaven for him; or ere I could

Give him that parting kiss which I had set

Betwixt two charming words, comes in my father,

And like the tyrannous breathing of the north

Shakes all our buds from growing.

Enter a Lady.

LADY.

The Queen, madam,

Desires your Highness' company.

IMOGEN.

Those things I bid you do, get them dispatch'd.

I will attend the Queen.

PISANIO.

Madam, I shall.

[Exeunt.]

SCENE V. Rome. Philario's house.

Enter Philario, Iachimo, a Frenchman, a Dutchman and a Spaniard.

IACHIMO.

Believe it, sir, I have seen him in Britain. He was then of a crescent note, expected to prove so worthy as since he hath been allowed the name of. But I could then have look'd on him without the help of admiration, though the catalogue of his endowments had been tabled by his side, and I to peruse him by items.

PHILARIO.

You speak of him when he was less furnish'd than now he is with that which makes him both without and within.

FRENCHMAN.

I have seen him in France; we had very many there could behold the sun with as firm eyes as he.

IACHIMO.

This matter of marrying his king's daughter, wherein he must be weighed rather by her value than his own, words him, I doubt not, a great deal from the matter.

FRENCHMAN.

And then his banishment.

IACHIMO.

Ay, and the approbation of those that weep this lamentable divorce under her colours are wonderfully to extend him, be it but to fortify her judgement, which else an easy battery might lay flat, for taking a beggar, without less quality. But how comes it he is to sojourn with you? How creeps acquaintance?

PHILARIO.

His father and I were soldiers together, to whom I have been often bound for no less than my life.

Enter Posthumus.

Here comes the Briton. Let him be so entertained amongst you as suits with gentlemen of your knowing to a stranger of his quality. I beseech you all be better known to this gentleman, whom I commend to you as a noble friend of mine. How worthy he is I will leave to appear hereafter, rather than story him in his own hearing.

FRENCHMAN.

Sir, we have known together in Orleans.

POSTHUMUS.

Since when I have been debtor to you for courtesies, which I will be ever to pay and yet pay still.

FRENCHMAN.

Sir, you o'errate my poor kindness. I was glad I did atone my countryman and you; it had been pity you should have been put together with so mortal a purpose as then each bore, upon importance of so slight and trivial a nature.

POSTHUMUS.

By your pardon, sir. I was then a young traveller; rather shunn'd to go even with what I heard than in my every action to be guided by others' experiences; but upon my mended judgement (if I offend not to say it is mended) my quarrel was not altogether slight.

FRENCHMAN.

Faith, yes, to be put to the arbitrement of swords, and by such two that would by all likelihood have confounded one the other or have fall'n both.

IACHIMO.

Can we, with manners, ask what was the difference?

FRENCHMAN.

Safely, I think. 'Twas a contention in public, which may, without contradiction, suffer the report. It was much like an argument that fell out last night, where each of us fell in praise of our country mistresses; this gentleman at that time vouching (and upon warrant of bloody affirmation) his to be more fair, virtuous, wise, chaste, constant, qualified, and less attemptable, than any the rarest of our ladies in France.

IACHIMO.

That lady is not now living, or this gentleman's opinion, by this, worn out.

POSTHUMUS.

She holds her virtue still, and I my mind.

IACHIMO.

You must not so far prefer her 'fore ours of Italy.

POSTHUMUS.

Being so far provok'd as I was in France, I would abate her nothing, though I profess myself her adorer, not her friend.

IACHIMO.

As fair and as good—a kind of hand-in-hand comparison—had been something too fair and too good for any lady in Britain. If she went before others I have seen as that diamond of yours outlustres many I have beheld, I could not but believe she excelled many; but I have not seen the most precious diamond that is, nor you the lady.

POSTHUMUS.

I prais'd her as I rated her. So do I my stone.

IACHIMO.

What do you esteem it at?

POSTHUMUS.

More than the world enjoys.

IACHIMO.

Either your unparagon'd mistress is dead, or she's outpriz'd by a trifle.

POSTHUMUS.

You are mistaken: the one may be sold or given, if there were wealth enough for the purchase or merit for the gift; the other is not a thing for sale, and only the gift of the gods.

IACHIMO.

Which the gods have given you?

POSTHUMUS.

Which by their graces I will keep.

IACHIMO.

You may wear her in title yours; but you know strange fowl light upon neighbouring ponds. Your ring may be stol'n too. So your brace of unprizable estimations, the one is but frail and the other casual; a cunning thief, or a that-way-accomplish'd courtier, would hazard the winning both of first and last.

POSTHUMUS.

Your Italy contains none so accomplish'd a courtier to convince the honour of my mistress, if in the holding or loss of that you term her frail. I do nothing doubt you have store of thieves; notwithstanding, I fear not my ring.

PHILARIO.

Let us leave here, gentlemen.

POSTHUMUS.

Sir, with all my heart. This worthy signior, I thank him, makes no stranger of me; we are familiar at first.

IACHIMO.

With five times so much conversation I should get ground of your fair mistress; make her go back even to the yielding, had I admittance and opportunity to friend.

POSTHUMUS.

No, no.

IACHIMO.

I dare thereupon pawn the moiety of my estate to your ring, which, in my opinion, o'ervalues it something. But I make my wager rather against your confidence than her reputation; and, to bar your offence herein too, I durst attempt it against any lady in the world.

POSTHUMUS.

You are a great deal abus'd in too bold a persuasion, and I doubt not you sustain what y'are worthy of by your attempt.

IACHIMO.

What's that?

POSTHUMUS.

A repulse; though your attempt, as you call it, deserve more; a punishment too.

PHILARIO.

Gentlemen, enough of this. It came in too suddenly; let it die as it was born, and I pray you be better acquainted.

IACHIMO.

Would I had put my estate and my neighbour's on th' approbation of what I have spoke!

POSTHUMUS.

What lady would you choose to assail?

IACHIMO.

Yours, whom in constancy you think stands so safe. I will lay you ten thousand ducats to your ring that, commend me to the court where your lady is, with no more advantage than the opportunity of a second conference, and I will bring from thence that honour of hers which you imagine so reserv'd.

POSTHUMUS.

I will wage against your gold, gold to it. My ring I hold dear as my finger; 'tis part of it.

IACHIMO.

You are a friend, and therein the wiser. If you buy ladies' flesh at a million a dram, you cannot preserve it from tainting. But I see you have some religion in you, that you fear.

POSTHUMUS.

This is but a custom in your tongue; you bear a graver purpose, I hope.

IACHIMO.

I am the master of my speeches, and would undergo what's spoken, I swear.

POSTHUMUS.

Will you? I shall but lend my diamond till your return. Let there be covenants drawn between's. My mistress exceeds in goodness the hugeness of your unworthy thinking. I dare you to this match: here's my ring.

PHILARIO.

I will have it no lay.

IACHIMO.

By the gods, it is one. If I bring you no sufficient testimony that I have enjoy'd the dearest bodily part of your mistress, my ten thousand ducats are yours; so is your diamond too. If I come off, and leave her in such honour as you have trust in, she your jewel, this your jewel, and my gold are yours: provided I have your commendation for my more free entertainment.

POSTHUMUS.

I embrace these conditions; let us have articles betwixt us. Only, thus far you shall answer: if you make your voyage upon her, and give me directly to understand you have prevail'd, I am no further your enemy; she is not worth our debate; if she remain unseduc'd, you not making it appear otherwise, for your ill opinion and th' assault you have made to her chastity you shall answer me with your sword.

IACHIMO.

Your hand, a covenant! We will have these things set down by lawful counsel, and straight away for Britain, lest the bargain should catch cold and starve. I will fetch my gold and have our two wagers recorded.

POSTHUMUS.

Agreed.

[Exeunt Posthumus and Iachimo.]

FRENCHMAN.

Will this hold, think you?

PHILARIO.

Signior Iachimo will not from it. Pray let us follow 'em.

[Exeunt.]

SCENE VI. Britain. Cymbeline's palace.

Enter Queen, Ladies and Cornelius.

QUEEN.

Whiles yet the dew's on ground, gather those flowers;

Make haste; who has the note of them?

LADY.

I, madam.

QUEEN.

Dispatch.

[Exeunt Ladies.]

Now, Master Doctor, have you brought those drugs?

CORNELIUS.

Pleaseth your Highness, ay. Here they are, madam.

[Presenting a box.]

But I beseech your Grace, without offence,

(My conscience bids me ask) wherefore you have

Commanded of me these most poisonous compounds

Which are the movers of a languishing death,

But, though slow, deadly?

QUEEN.

I wonder, Doctor,

Thou ask'st me such a question. Have I not been

Thy pupil long? Hast thou not learn'd me how

To make perfumes? distil? preserve? yea, so

That our great king himself doth woo me oft

For my confections? Having thus far proceeded

(Unless thou think'st me devilish) is't not meet

That I did amplify my judgement in

Other conclusions? I will try the forces

Of these thy compounds on such creatures as

We count not worth the hanging (but none human)

To try the vigour of them, and apply

Allayments to their act, and by them gather

Their several virtues and effects.

CORNELIUS.

Your Highness

Shall from this practice but make hard your heart;

Besides, the seeing these effects will be

Both noisome and infectious.

QUEEN.

O, content thee.

Enter Pisanio.

[Aside.] Here comes a flattering rascal; upon him

Will I first work. He's for his master,

An enemy to my son. How now, Pisanio!

Doctor, your service for this time is ended;

Take your own way.

CORNELIUS.

[Aside.] I do suspect you, madam;

But you shall do no harm.

QUEEN.

[To Pisanio.] Hark thee, a word.

CORNELIUS.

[Aside.] I do not like her. She doth think she has

Strange ling'ring poisons. I do know her spirit,

And will not trust one of her malice with

A drug of such damn'd nature. Those she has

Will stupefy and dull the sense awhile,

Which first perchance she'll prove on cats and dogs,

Then afterward up higher; but there is

No danger in what show of death it makes,

More than the locking up the spirits a time,

To be more fresh, reviving. She is fool'd

With a most false effect; and I the truer

So to be false with her.

QUEEN.

No further service, Doctor,

Until I send for thee.

CORNELIUS.

I humbly take my leave.

[Exit.]

QUEEN.

Weeps she still, say'st thou? Dost thou think in time

She will not quench, and let instructions enter

Where folly now possesses? Do thou work.

When thou shalt bring me word she loves my son,

I'll tell thee on the instant thou art then

As great as is thy master; greater, for

His fortunes all lie speechless, and his name

Is at last gasp. Return he cannot, nor

Continue where he is. To shift his being

Is to exchange one misery with another,

And every day that comes comes to decay

A day's work in him. What shalt thou expect

To be depender on a thing that leans,

Who cannot be new built, nor has no friends

So much as but to prop him?

[The Queen drops the box. Pisanio takes it up.]

Thou tak'st up

Thou know'st not what; but take it for thy labour.

It is a thing I made, which hath the King

Five times redeem'd from death. I do not know

What is more cordial. Nay, I prithee take it;

It is an earnest of a further good

That I mean to thee. Tell thy mistress how

The case stands with her; do't as from thyself.

Think what a chance thou changest on; but think

Thou hast thy mistress still; to boot, my son,

Who shall take notice of thee. I'll move the King

To any shape of thy preferment, such

As thou'lt desire; and then myself, I chiefly,

That set thee on to this desert, am bound

To load thy merit richly. Call my women.

Think on my words.

[Exit Pisanio.]

A sly and constant knave,

Not to be shak'd; the agent for his master,

And the remembrancer of her to hold

The hand-fast to her lord. I have given him that

Which, if he take, shall quite unpeople her

Of liegers for her sweet; and which she after,

Except she bend her humour, shall be assur'd

To taste of too.

Enter Pisanio and Ladies.

So, so. Well done, well done.

The violets, cowslips, and the primroses,

Bear to my closet. Fare thee well, Pisanio;

Think on my words.

[Exeunt Queen and Ladies.]

PISANIO.

And shall do.

But when to my good lord I prove untrue

I'll choke myself: there's all I'll do for you.

[Exit.]

SCENE VII. Britain. The palace.

Enter Imogen alone.

IMOGEN.

A father cruel and a step-dame false;

A foolish suitor to a wedded lady

That hath her husband banish'd. O, that husband!

My supreme crown of grief! and those repeated

Vexations of it! Had I been thief-stol'n,

As my two brothers, happy! but most miserable

Is the desire that's glorious. Blessed be those,

How mean soe'er, that have their honest wills,

Which seasons comfort. Who may this be? Fie!

Enter Pisanio and Iachimo.

PISANIO.

Madam, a noble gentleman of Rome

Comes from my lord with letters.

IACHIMO.

Change you, madam?

The worthy Leonatus is in safety,

And greets your Highness dearly.

[Presents a letter.]

IMOGEN.

Thanks, good sir.

You're kindly welcome.

IACHIMO.

[Aside.] All of her that is out of door most rich!

If she be furnish'd with a mind so rare,

She is alone th' Arabian bird, and I

Have lost the wager. Boldness be my friend!

Arm me, audacity, from head to foot!

Or, like the Parthian, I shall flying fight;

Rather, directly fly.

IMOGEN.

[Reads.] He is one of the noblest note, to whose kindnesses I am most infinitely tied. Reflect upon him accordingly, as you value your trust.

LEONATUS.

So far I read aloud;

But even the very middle of my heart

Is warm'd by th' rest and takes it thankfully.

You are as welcome, worthy sir, as I

Have words to bid you; and shall find it so

In all that I can do.

IACHIMO.

Thanks, fairest lady.

What, are men mad? Hath nature given them eyes

To see this vaulted arch and the rich crop

Of sea and land, which can distinguish 'twixt

The fiery orbs above and the twinn'd stones

Upon the number'd beach, and can we not

Partition make with spectacles so precious

'Twixt fair and foul?

IMOGEN.

What makes your admiration?

IACHIMO.

It cannot be i' th' eye, for apes and monkeys,

'Twixt two such shes, would chatter this way and

Contemn with mows the other; nor i' th' judgement,

For idiots in this case of favour would

Be wisely definite; nor i' th' appetite;

Sluttery, to such neat excellence oppos'd,

Should make desire vomit emptiness,

Not so allur'd to feed.

IMOGEN.

What is the matter, trow?

IACHIMO.

The cloyed will—

That satiate yet unsatisfied desire, that tub

Both fill'd and running—ravening first the lamb,

Longs after for the garbage.

IMOGEN.

What, dear sir,

Thus raps you? Are you well?

IACHIMO.

Thanks, madam; well. Beseech you, sir,

Desire my man's abode where I did leave him.

He's strange and peevish.

PISANIO.

I was going, sir,

To give him welcome.

[Exit.]

IMOGEN.

Continues well my lord? His health beseech you?

IACHIMO.

Well, madam.

IMOGEN.

Is he dispos'd to mirth? I hope he is.

IACHIMO.

Exceeding pleasant; none a stranger there

So merry and so gamesome. He is call'd

The Briton reveller.

IMOGEN.

When he was here

He did incline to sadness, and oft-times

Not knowing why.

IACHIMO.

I never saw him sad.

There is a Frenchman his companion, one

An eminent monsieur that, it seems, much loves

A Gallian girl at home. He furnaces

The thick sighs from him; whiles the jolly Briton

(Your lord, I mean) laughs from's free lungs, cries "O,

Can my sides hold, to think that man, who knows

By history, report, or his own proof,

What woman is, yea, what she cannot choose

But must be, will's free hours languish for

Assured bondage?"

IMOGEN.

Will my lord say so?

IACHIMO.

Ay, madam, with his eyes in flood with laughter.

It is a recreation to be by

And hear him mock the Frenchman. But heavens know

Some men are much to blame.

IMOGEN.

Not he, I hope.

IACHIMO.

Not he; but yet heaven's bounty towards him might

Be us'd more thankfully. In himself, 'tis much;

In you, which I account his, beyond all talents.

Whilst I am bound to wonder, I am bound

To pity too.

IMOGEN.

What do you pity, sir?

IACHIMO.

Two creatures heartily.

IMOGEN.

Am I one, sir?

You look on me: what wreck discern you in me

Deserves your pity?

IACHIMO.

Lamentable! What,

To hide me from the radiant sun and solace

I' th' dungeon by a snuff?

IMOGEN.

I pray you, sir,

Deliver with more openness your answers

To my demands. Why do you pity me?

IACHIMO.

That others do,

I was about to say, enjoy your—But

It is an office of the gods to venge it,

Not mine to speak on't.

IMOGEN.

You do seem to know

Something of me, or what concerns me; pray you,

Since doubting things go ill often hurts more

Than to be sure they do; for certainties

Either are past remedies, or, timely knowing,

The remedy then born—discover to me

What both you spur and stop.

IACHIMO.

Had I this cheek

To bathe my lips upon; this hand, whose touch,

Whose every touch, would force the feeler's soul

To th' oath of loyalty; this object, which

Takes prisoner the wild motion of mine eye,

Fixing it only here; should I, damn'd then,

Slaver with lips as common as the stairs

That mount the Capitol; join gripes with hands

Made hard with hourly falsehood (falsehood as

With labour): then by-peeping in an eye

Base and illustrious as the smoky light

That's fed with stinking tallow: it were fit

That all the plagues of hell should at one time

Encounter such revolt.

IMOGEN.

My lord, I fear,

Has forgot Britain.

IACHIMO.

And himself. Not I

Inclin'd to this intelligence pronounce

The beggary of his change; but 'tis your graces

That from my mutest conscience to my tongue

Charms this report out.

IMOGEN.

Let me hear no more.

IACHIMO.

O dearest soul, your cause doth strike my heart

With pity that doth make me sick! A lady

So fair, and fasten'd to an empery,

Would make the great'st king double, to be partner'd

With tomboys hir'd with that self exhibition

Which your own coffers yield! with diseas'd ventures

That play with all infirmities for gold

Which rottenness can lend nature! Such boil'd stuff

As well might poison poison! Be reveng'd;

Or she that bore you was no queen, and you

Recoil from your great stock.

IMOGEN.

Reveng'd?

How should I be reveng'd? If this be true,

(As I have such a heart that both mine ears

Must not in haste abuse) if it be true,

How should I be reveng'd?

IACHIMO.

Should he make me

Live like Diana's priest betwixt cold sheets,

Whiles he is vaulting variable ramps,

In your despite, upon your purse? Revenge it.

I dedicate myself to your sweet pleasure,

More noble than that runagate to your bed,

And will continue fast to your affection,

Still close as sure.

IMOGEN.

What ho, Pisanio!

IACHIMO.

Let me my service tender on your lips.

IMOGEN.

Away! I do condemn mine ears that have

So long attended thee. If thou wert honourable,

Thou wouldst have told this tale for virtue, not

For such an end thou seek'st, as base as strange.

Thou wrong'st a gentleman who is as far

From thy report as thou from honour; and

Solicits here a lady that disdains

Thee and the devil alike. What ho, Pisanio!

The King my father shall be made acquainted

Of thy assault. If he shall think it fit

A saucy stranger in his court to mart

As in a Romish stew, and to expound

His beastly mind to us, he hath a court

He little cares for, and a daughter who

He not respects at all. What ho, Pisanio!

IACHIMO.

O happy Leonatus! I may say

The credit that thy lady hath of thee

Deserves thy trust, and thy most perfect goodness

Her assur'd credit. Blessed live you long,

A lady to the worthiest sir that ever

Country call'd his! and you his mistress, only

For the most worthiest fit! Give me your pardon.

I have spoke this to know if your affiance

Were deeply rooted, and shall make your lord

That which he is new o'er; and he is one

The truest manner'd, such a holy witch

That he enchants societies into him,

Half all men's hearts are his.

IMOGEN.

You make amends.

IACHIMO.

He sits 'mongst men like a descended god:

He hath a kind of honour sets him off

More than a mortal seeming. Be not angry,

Most mighty Princess, that I have adventur'd

To try your taking of a false report, which hath

Honour'd with confirmation your great judgement

In the election of a sir so rare,

Which you know cannot err. The love I bear him

Made me to fan you thus; but the gods made you,

Unlike all others, chaffless. Pray your pardon.

IMOGEN.

All's well, sir; take my pow'r i' th' court for yours.

IACHIMO.

My humble thanks. I had almost forgot

T' entreat your Grace but in a small request,

And yet of moment too, for it concerns

Your lord; myself and other noble friends

Are partners in the business.

IMOGEN.

Pray what is't?

IACHIMO.

Some dozen Romans of us, and your lord

(The best feather of our wing) have mingled sums

To buy a present for the Emperor;

Which I, the factor for the rest, have done

In France. 'Tis plate of rare device, and jewels

Of rich and exquisite form, their values great;

And I am something curious, being strange,

To have them in safe stowage. May it please you

To take them in protection?

IMOGEN.

Willingly;

And pawn mine honour for their safety. Since

My lord hath interest in them, I will keep them

In my bedchamber.

IACHIMO.

They are in a trunk,

Attended by my men. I will make bold

To send them to you only for this night;

I must aboard tomorrow.

IMOGEN.

O, no, no.

IACHIMO.

Yes, I beseech; or I shall short my word

By length'ning my return. From Gallia

I cross'd the seas on purpose and on promise

To see your Grace.

IMOGEN.

I thank you for your pains.

But not away tomorrow!

IACHIMO.

O, I must, madam.

Therefore I shall beseech you, if you please

To greet your lord with writing, do't tonight.

I have outstood my time, which is material

To th' tender of our present.

IMOGEN.

I will write.

Send your trunk to me; it shall safe be kept

And truly yielded you. You're very welcome.

[Exeunt.]

ACT II

SCENE I. Britain. Before Cymbeline's palace.

Enter Cloten and the two Lords.

CLOTEN.

Was there ever man had such luck! When I kiss'd the jack, upon an upcast to be hit away! I had a hundred pound on't; and then a whoreson jackanapes must take me up for swearing, as if I borrowed mine oaths of him, and might not spend them at my pleasure.

FIRST LORD.

What got he by that? You have broke his pate with your bowl.

SECOND LORD.

[Aside.] If his wit had been like him that broke it, it would have run all out.

CLOTEN.

When a gentleman is dispos'd to swear, it is not for any standers-by to curtail his oaths. Ha?

SECOND LORD.

No, my lord; [Aside.] nor crop the ears of them.

CLOTEN.

Whoreson dog! I gave him satisfaction. Would he had been one of my rank!

SECOND LORD.

[Aside.] To have smell'd like a fool.

CLOTEN.

I am not vex'd more at anything in th' earth. A pox on't! I had rather not be so noble as I am; they dare not fight with me, because of the Queen my mother. Every jackslave hath his bellyful of fighting, and I must go up and down like a cock that nobody can match.

SECOND LORD.

[Aside.] You are cock and capon too; and you crow, cock, with your comb on.

CLOTEN.

Sayest thou?

SECOND LORD.

It is not fit your lordship should undertake every companion that you give offence to.

CLOTEN.

No, I know that; but it is fit I should commit offence to my inferiors.

SECOND LORD.

Ay, it is fit for your lordship only.

CLOTEN.

Why, so I say.

FIRST LORD.

Did you hear of a stranger that's come to court tonight?

CLOTEN.

A stranger, and I not known on't?

SECOND LORD.

[Aside.] He's a strange fellow himself, and knows it not.

FIRST LORD.

There's an Italian come, and, 'tis thought, one of Leonatus' friends.

CLOTEN.

Leonatus? A banish'd rascal; and he's another, whatsoever he be. Who told you of this stranger?

FIRST LORD.

One of your lordship's pages.

CLOTEN.

Is it fit I went to look upon him? Is there no derogation in't?

SECOND LORD.

You cannot derogate, my lord.

CLOTEN.

Not easily, I think.

SECOND LORD.

[Aside.] You are a fool granted; therefore your issues, being foolish, do not derogate.

CLOTEN.

Come, I'll go see this Italian. What I have lost today at bowls I'll win tonight of him. Come, go.

SECOND LORD.

I'll attend your lordship.

[Exeunt Cloten and First Lord.]

That such a crafty devil as is his mother

Should yield the world this ass! A woman that

Bears all down with her brain; and this her son

Cannot take two from twenty, for his heart,

And leave eighteen. Alas, poor princess,

Thou divine Imogen, what thou endur'st,

Betwixt a father by thy step-dame govern'd,

A mother hourly coining plots, a wooer

More hateful than the foul expulsion is

Of thy dear husband, than that horrid act

Of the divorce he'd make! The heavens hold firm

The walls of thy dear honour, keep unshak'd

That temple, thy fair mind, that thou mayst stand

T' enjoy thy banish'd lord and this great land!

[Exit.]

SCENE II. Britain. Imogen's bedchamber in Cymbeline's palace; a trunk in one corner.

Enter Immogen in her bed, and a Lady attending.

IMOGEN.

Who's there? My woman Helen?

LADY.

Please you, madam.

IMOGEN.

What hour is it?

LADY.

Almost midnight, madam.

IMOGEN.

I have read three hours then. Mine eyes are weak;

Fold down the leaf where I have left. To bed.

Take not away the taper, leave it burning;

And if thou canst awake by four o' th' clock,

I prithee call me. Sleep hath seiz'd me wholly.

[Exit Lady.]

To your protection I commend me, gods.

From fairies and the tempters of the night

Guard me, beseech ye!

[Sleeps. Iachimo comes from the trunk.]

IACHIMO.

The crickets sing, and man's o'er-labour'd sense

Repairs itself by rest. Our Tarquin thus

Did softly press the rushes ere he waken'd

The chastity he wounded. Cytherea,

How bravely thou becom'st thy bed! fresh lily,

And whiter than the sheets! That I might touch!

But kiss; one kiss! Rubies unparagon'd,

How dearly they do't! 'Tis her breathing that

Perfumes the chamber thus. The flame o' th' taper

Bows toward her and would under-peep her lids

To see th' enclosed lights, now canopied

Under these windows white and azure, lac'd

With blue of heaven's own tinct. But my design

To note the chamber. I will write all down:

Such and such pictures; there the window; such

Th' adornment of her bed; the arras, figures,

Why, such and such; and the contents o' th' story.

Ah, but some natural notes about her body

Above ten thousand meaner movables

Would testify, t' enrich mine inventory.

O sleep, thou ape of death, lie dull upon her!

And be her sense but as a monument,

Thus in a chapel lying! Come off, come off;

[Taking off her bracelet.]

As slippery as the Gordian knot was hard!

'Tis mine; and this will witness outwardly,

As strongly as the conscience does within,

To th' madding of her lord. On her left breast

A mole cinque-spotted, like the crimson drops

I' th' bottom of a cowslip. Here's a voucher

Stronger than ever law could make; this secret

Will force him think I have pick'd the lock and ta'en

The treasure of her honour. No more. To what end?

Why should I write this down that's riveted,

Screw'd to my memory? She hath been reading late

The tale of Tereus; here the leaf's turn'd down

Where Philomel gave up. I have enough.

To th' trunk again, and shut the spring of it.

Swift, swift, you dragons of the night, that dawning

May bare the raven's eye! I lodge in fear;

Though this a heavenly angel, hell is here.

[Clock strikes.]

One, two, three. Time, time!

[Exit into the trunk.]

SCENE III. Cymbeline's palace. An ante-chamber adjoining Imogen's apartments.

Enter Cloten and Lords.

FIRST LORD.

Your lordship is the most patient man in loss, the most coldest that ever turn'd up ace.

CLOTEN.

It would make any man cold to lose.

FIRST LORD.

But not every man patient after the noble temper of your lordship. You are most hot and furious when you win.

CLOTEN.

Winning will put any man into courage. If I could get this foolish Imogen, I should have gold enough. It's almost morning, is't not?

FIRST LORD.

Day, my lord.

CLOTEN.

I would this music would come. I am advised to give her music a mornings; they say it will penetrate.

Enter Musicians.

Come on, tune. If you can penetrate her with your fingering, so. We'll try with tongue too. If none will do, let her remain; but I'll never give o'er. First, a very excellent good-conceited thing; after, a wonderful sweet air, with admirable rich words to it, and then let her consider.

SONG

Hark, hark! the lark at heaven's gate sings,

And Phœbus 'gins arise,

His steeds to water at those springs

On chalic'd flow'rs that lies;

And winking Mary-buds begin

To ope their golden eyes.

With everything that pretty is,

My lady sweet, arise;

Arise, arise!

CLOTEN.

So, get you gone. If this penetrate, I will consider your music the better; if it do not, it is a vice in her ears which horsehairs and calves' guts, nor the voice of unpaved eunuch to boot, can never amend.

[Exeunt Musicians.]

Enter Cymbeline and Queen.

SECOND LORD.

Here comes the King.

CLOTEN.

I am glad I was up so late, for that's the reason I was up so early. He cannot choose but take this service I have done fatherly.—Good morrow to your Majesty and to my gracious mother.

CYMBELINE.

Attend you here the door of our stern daughter?

Will she not forth?

CLOTEN.

I have assail'd her with musics, but she vouchsafes no notice.

CYMBELINE.

The exile of her minion is too new;

She hath not yet forgot him; some more time

Must wear the print of his remembrance on't,

And then she's yours.

QUEEN.

You are most bound to th' King,

Who lets go by no vantages that may

Prefer you to his daughter. Frame yourself

To orderly solicits, and be friended

With aptness of the season; make denials

Increase your services; so seem as if

You were inspir'd to do those duties which

You tender to her; that you in all obey her,

Save when command to your dismission tends,

And therein you are senseless.

CLOTEN.

Senseless? Not so.

Enter a Messenger.

MESSENGER.

So like you, sir, ambassadors from Rome;

The one is Caius Lucius.

CYMBELINE.

A worthy fellow,

Albeit he comes on angry purpose now;

But that's no fault of his. We must receive him

According to the honour of his sender;

And towards himself, his goodness forespent on us,

We must extend our notice. Our dear son,

When you have given good morning to your mistress,

Attend the Queen and us; we shall have need

T' employ you towards this Roman. Come, our queen.

[Exeunt all but Cloten.]

CLOTEN.

If she be up, I'll speak with her; if not,

Let her lie still and dream. By your leave, ho!

[Knocks.]

I know her women are about her; what

If I do line one of their hands? 'Tis gold

Which buys admittance (oft it doth) yea, and makes

Diana's rangers false themselves, yield up

Their deer to th' stand o' th' stealer; and 'tis gold

Which makes the true man kill'd and saves the thief;

Nay, sometime hangs both thief and true man. What

Can it not do and undo? I will make

One of her women lawyer to me, for

I yet not understand the case myself.

By your leave.

[Knocks.]

Enter a Lady.

LADY.

Who's there that knocks?

CLOTEN.

A gentleman.

LADY.

No more?

CLOTEN.

Yes, and a gentlewoman's son.

LADY.

That's more

Than some whose tailors are as dear as yours

Can justly boast of. What's your lordship's pleasure?

CLOTEN.

Your lady's person; is she ready?

LADY.

Ay,

To keep her chamber.

CLOTEN.

There is gold for you; sell me your good report.

LADY.

How? My good name? or to report of you

What I shall think is good? The Princess!

Enter Imogen.

CLOTEN.

Good morrow, fairest sister. Your sweet hand.

[Exit Lady.]

IMOGEN.

Good morrow, sir. You lay out too much pains

For purchasing but trouble. The thanks I give

Is telling you that I am poor of thanks,

And scarce can spare them.

CLOTEN.

Still I swear I love you.

IMOGEN.

If you but said so, 'twere as deep with me.

If you swear still, your recompense is still

That I regard it not.

CLOTEN.

This is no answer.

IMOGEN.

But that you shall not say I yield, being silent,

I would not speak. I pray you spare me. Faith,

I shall unfold equal discourtesy

To your best kindness; one of your great knowing

Should learn, being taught, forbearance.

CLOTEN.

To leave you in your madness 'twere my sin;

I will not.

IMOGEN.

Fools are not mad folks.

CLOTEN.

Do you call me fool?

IMOGEN.

As I am mad, I do;

If you'll be patient, I'll no more be mad;

That cures us both. I am much sorry, sir,

You put me to forget a lady's manners

By being so verbal; and learn now, for all,

That I, which know my heart, do here pronounce,

By th' very truth of it, I care not for you,

And am so near the lack of charity

To accuse myself I hate you; which I had rather

You felt than make't my boast.

CLOTEN.

You sin against

Obedience, which you owe your father. For

The contract you pretend with that base wretch,

One bred of alms and foster'd with cold dishes,

With scraps o' th' court, it is no contract, none.

And though it be allowed in meaner parties

(Yet who than he more mean?) to knit their souls

(On whom there is no more dependency

But brats and beggary) in self-figur'd knot,

Yet you are curb'd from that enlargement by

The consequence o' th' crown, and must not foil

The precious note of it with a base slave,

A hilding for a livery, a squire's cloth,

A pantler; not so eminent!

IMOGEN.

Profane fellow!

Wert thou the son of Jupiter, and no more

But what thou art besides, thou wert too base

To be his groom. Thou wert dignified enough,

Even to the point of envy, if 'twere made

Comparative for your virtues to be styl'd

The under-hangman of his kingdom, and hated

For being preferr'd so well.

CLOTEN.

The south fog rot him!

IMOGEN.

He never can meet more mischance than come

To be but nam'd of thee. His mean'st garment

That ever hath but clipp'd his body, is dearer

In my respect, than all the hairs above thee,

Were they all made such men. How now, Pisanio!

Enter Pisanio.

CLOTEN.

'His garment'! Now the devil—

IMOGEN.

To Dorothy my woman hie thee presently.

CLOTEN.

'His garment'!

IMOGEN.

I am sprited with a fool;

Frighted, and ang'red worse. Go bid my woman

Search for a jewel that too casually

Hath left mine arm. It was thy master's; shrew me,

If I would lose it for a revenue

Of any king's in Europe! I do think

I saw't this morning; confident I am

Last night 'twas on mine arm; I kiss'd it.

I hope it be not gone to tell my lord

That I kiss aught but he.

PISANIO.

'Twill not be lost.

IMOGEN.

I hope so. Go and search.

[Exit Pisanio.]

CLOTEN.

You have abus'd me.

'His meanest garment'!

IMOGEN.

Ay, I said so, sir.

If you will make 't an action, call witness to 't.

CLOTEN.

I will inform your father.

IMOGEN.

Your mother too.

She's my good lady and will conceive, I hope,

But the worst of me. So I leave you, sir,

To th' worst of discontent.

[Exit.]

CLOTEN.

I'll be reveng'd.

'His mean'st garment'! Well.

[Exit.]

SCENE IV. Rome. Philario's house.

Enter Posthumus and Philario.

POSTHUMUS.

Fear it not, sir; I would I were so sure

To win the King as I am bold her honour

Will remain hers.

PHILARIO.

What means do you make to him?

POSTHUMUS.

Not any; but abide the change of time,

Quake in the present winter's state, and wish

That warmer days would come. In these fear'd hopes

I barely gratify your love; they failing,

I must die much your debtor.

PHILARIO.

Your very goodness and your company

O'erpays all I can do. By this your king

Hath heard of great Augustus. Caius Lucius

Will do's commission throughly; and I think

He'll grant the tribute, send th' arrearages,

Or look upon our Romans, whose remembrance

Is yet fresh in their grief.

POSTHUMUS.

I do believe

Statist though I am none, nor like to be,

That this will prove a war; and you shall hear

The legions now in Gallia sooner landed

In our not-fearing Britain than have tidings

Of any penny tribute paid. Our countrymen

Are men more order'd than when Julius Cæsar

Smil'd at their lack of skill, but found their courage

Worthy his frowning at. Their discipline,

Now mingled with their courages, will make known

To their approvers they are people such

That mend upon the world.

Enter Iachimo.

PHILARIO.

See! Iachimo!

POSTHUMUS.

The swiftest harts have posted you by land,

And winds of all the corners kiss'd your sails,

To make your vessel nimble.

PHILARIO.

Welcome, sir.

POSTHUMUS.

I hope the briefness of your answer made

The speediness of your return.

IACHIMO.

Your lady

Is one of the fairest that I have look'd upon.

POSTHUMUS.

And therewithal the best; or let her beauty

Look through a casement to allure false hearts,

And be false with them.

IACHIMO.

Here are letters for you.

POSTHUMUS.

Their tenour good, I trust.

IACHIMO.

'Tis very like.

PHILARIO.

Was Caius Lucius in the Britain court

When you were there?

IACHIMO.

He was expected then,

But not approach'd.

POSTHUMUS.

All is well yet.

Sparkles this stone as it was wont, or is't not

Too dull for your good wearing?

IACHIMO.

If I have lost it,

I should have lost the worth of it in gold.

I'll make a journey twice as far t' enjoy

A second night of such sweet shortness which

Was mine in Britain; for the ring is won.

POSTHUMUS.

The stone's too hard to come by.

IACHIMO.

Not a whit,

Your lady being so easy.

POSTHUMUS.

Make not, sir,

Your loss your sport. I hope you know that we

Must not continue friends.

IACHIMO.

Good sir, we must,

If you keep covenant. Had I not brought

The knowledge of your mistress home, I grant

We were to question farther; but I now

Profess myself the winner of her honour,

Together with your ring; and not the wronger

Of her or you, having proceeded but

By both your wills.

POSTHUMUS.

If you can make't apparent

That you have tasted her in bed, my hand

And ring is yours. If not, the foul opinion

You had of her pure honour gains or loses

Your sword or mine, or masterless leaves both

To who shall find them.

IACHIMO.

Sir, my circumstances,

Being so near the truth as I will make them,

Must first induce you to believe; whose strength

I will confirm with oath; which I doubt not

You'll give me leave to spare when you shall find

You need it not.

POSTHUMUS.

Proceed.

IACHIMO.

First, her bedchamber,

(Where I confess I slept not, but profess

Had that was well worth watching) it was hang'd

With tapestry of silk and silver; the story,

Proud Cleopatra when she met her Roman

And Cydnus swell'd above the banks, or for

The press of boats or pride. A piece of work

So bravely done, so rich, that it did strive

In workmanship and value; which I wonder'd

Could be so rarely and exactly wrought,

Since the true life on't was—

POSTHUMUS.

This is true;

And this you might have heard of here, by me

Or by some other.

IACHIMO.

More particulars

Must justify my knowledge.

POSTHUMUS.

So they must,

Or do your honour injury.

IACHIMO.

The chimney

Is south the chamber, and the chimneypiece

Chaste Dian bathing. Never saw I figures

So likely to report themselves. The cutter

Was as another nature, dumb; outwent her,

Motion and breath left out.

POSTHUMUS.

This is a thing

Which you might from relation likewise reap,

Being, as it is, much spoke of.

IACHIMO.

The roof o' th' chamber

With golden cherubins is fretted; her andirons

(I had forgot them) were two winking Cupids

Of silver, each on one foot standing, nicely

Depending on their brands.

POSTHUMUS.

This is her honour!

Let it be granted you have seen all this, and praise

Be given to your remembrance; the description

Of what is in her chamber nothing saves

The wager you have laid.

IACHIMO.

Then, if you can, [Shows the bracelet]

Be pale. I beg but leave to air this jewel. See!

And now 'tis up again. It must be married

To that your diamond; I'll keep them.

POSTHUMUS.

Jove!

Once more let me behold it. Is it that

Which I left with her?

IACHIMO.

Sir (I thank her) that.

She stripp'd it from her arm; I see her yet;

Her pretty action did outsell her gift,

And yet enrich'd it too. She gave it me, and said

She priz'd it once.

POSTHUMUS.

May be she pluck'd it of

To send it me.

IACHIMO.

She writes so to you, doth she?

POSTHUMUS.

O, no, no, no! 'tis true. Here, take this too;

[Gives the ring.]

It is a basilisk unto mine eye,

Kills me to look on't. Let there be no honour

Where there is beauty; truth where semblance; love

Where there's another man. The vows of women

Of no more bondage be to where they are made

Than they are to their virtues, which is nothing.

O, above measure false!

PHILARIO.

Have patience, sir,

And take your ring again; 'tis not yet won.

It may be probable she lost it, or

Who knows if one her women, being corrupted

Hath stol'n it from her?

POSTHUMUS.

Very true;

And so I hope he came by't. Back my ring.

Render to me some corporal sign about her,

More evident than this; for this was stol'n.

IACHIMO.

By Jupiter, I had it from her arm!

POSTHUMUS.

Hark you, he swears; by Jupiter he swears.

'Tis true, nay, keep the ring, 'tis true. I am sure

She would not lose it. Her attendants are

All sworn and honourable:—they induc'd to steal it!

And by a stranger! No, he hath enjoy'd her.

The cognizance of her incontinency

Is this: she hath bought the name of whore thus dearly.

There, take thy hire; and all the fiends of hell

Divide themselves between you!

PHILARIO.

Sir, be patient;

This is not strong enough to be believ'd

Of one persuaded well of.

POSTHUMUS.

Never talk on't;

She hath been colted by him.

IACHIMO.

If you seek

For further satisfying, under her breast

(Worthy the pressing) lies a mole, right proud

Of that most delicate lodging. By my life,

I kiss'd it; and it gave me present hunger

To feed again, though full. You do remember

This stain upon her?

POSTHUMUS.

Ay, and it doth confirm

Another stain, as big as hell can hold,

Were there no more but it.

IACHIMO.

Will you hear more?

POSTHUMUS.

Spare your arithmetic; never count the turns.

Once, and a million!

IACHIMO.

I'll be sworn—

POSTHUMUS.

No swearing.

If you will swear you have not done't, you lie;

And I will kill thee if thou dost deny

Thou'st made me cuckold.

IACHIMO.

I'll deny nothing.

POSTHUMUS.

O that I had her here to tear her limb-meal!

I will go there and do't, i' th' court, before

Her father. I'll do something—

[Exit.]

PHILARIO.

Quite besides

The government of patience! You have won.

Let's follow him and pervert the present wrath

He hath against himself.

IACHIMO.

With all my heart.

[Exeunt.]

SCENE V. Rome. Another room in Philario's house.

Enter Posthumus.

POSTHUMUS.

Is there no way for men to be, but women

Must be half-workers? We are all bastards,

And that most venerable man which I

Did call my father was I know not where

When I was stamp'd. Some coiner with his tools

Made me a counterfeit; yet my mother seem'd

The Dian of that time. So doth my wife

The nonpareil of this. O, vengeance, vengeance!

Me of my lawful pleasure she restrain'd,

And pray'd me oft forbearance; did it with

A pudency so rosy, the sweet view on't

Might well have warm'd old Saturn; that I thought her

As chaste as unsunn'd snow. O, all the devils!

This yellow Iachimo in an hour, was't not?

Or less; at first? Perchance he spoke not, but,

Like a full-acorn'd boar, a German one,

Cried "O!" and mounted; found no opposition

But what he look'd for should oppose and she

Should from encounter guard. Could I find out

The woman's part in me! For there's no motion

That tends to vice in man but I affirm

It is the woman's part. Be it lying, note it,

The woman's; flattering, hers; deceiving, hers;

Lust and rank thoughts, hers, hers; revenges, hers;

Ambitions, covetings, change of prides, disdain,

Nice longing, slanders, mutability,

All faults that man may name, nay, that hell knows,

Why, hers, in part or all; but rather all;

For even to vice

They are not constant, but are changing still

One vice but of a minute old for one

Not half so old as that. I'll write against them,

Detest them, curse them. Yet 'tis greater skill

In a true hate to pray they have their will:

The very devils cannot plague them better.

[Exit.]

ACT III

SCENE I. Britain. A hall in Cymbeline's palace.

Enter in state Cymbeline, Queen, Cloten and Lords at one door, and at another Caius Lucius and Attendants.

CYMBELINE.

Now say, what would Augustus Cæsar with us?

LUCIUS.

When Julius Cæsar, (whose remembrance yet

Lives in men's eyes, and will to ears and tongues

Be theme and hearing ever) was in this Britain,

And conquer'd it, Cassibelan, thine uncle,

Famous in Cæsar's praises no whit less

Than in his feats deserving it, for him

And his succession granted Rome a tribute,

Yearly three thousand pounds, which by thee lately

Is left untender'd.

QUEEN.

And, to kill the marvel,

Shall be so ever.

CLOTEN.

There be many Cæsars ere such another Julius. Britain is a world by itself, and we will nothing pay for wearing our own noses.

QUEEN.

That opportunity,

Which then they had to take from's, to resume

We have again. Remember, sir, my liege,

The kings your ancestors, together with

The natural bravery of your isle, which stands

As Neptune's park, ribb'd and pal'd in

With rocks unscaleable and roaring waters,

With sands that will not bear your enemies' boats

But suck them up to th' top-mast. A kind of conquest

Cæsar made here, but made not here his brag

Of 'Came, and saw, and overcame.' With shame

(The first that ever touch'd him) he was carried

From off our coast, twice beaten; and his shipping

(Poor ignorant baubles!) on our terrible seas,

Like egg-shells mov'd upon their surges, crack'd

As easily 'gainst our rocks; for joy whereof

The fam'd Cassibelan, who was once at point

(O, giglot fortune!) to master Cæsar's sword,

Made Lud's Town with rejoicing fires bright

And Britons strut with courage.

CLOTEN.

Come, there's no more tribute to be paid. Our kingdom is stronger than it was at that time; and, as I said, there is no moe such Cæsars. Other of them may have crook'd noses; but to owe such straight arms, none.

CYMBELINE.

Son, let your mother end.

CLOTEN.

We have yet many among us can gripe as hard as Cassibelan. I do not say I am one; but I have a hand. Why tribute? Why should we pay tribute? If Cæsar can hide the sun from us with a blanket, or put the moon in his pocket, we will pay him tribute for light; else, sir, no more tribute, pray you now.

CYMBELINE.

You must know,

Till the injurious Romans did extort

This tribute from us, we were free. Cæsar's ambition,

Which swell'd so much that it did almost stretch

The sides o' th' world, against all colour here

Did put the yoke upon's; which to shake of

Becomes a warlike people, whom we reckon

Ourselves to be.

CLOTEN.

We do.

CYMBELINE.

Say then to Cæsar,

Our ancestor was that Mulmutius which

Ordain'd our laws, whose use the sword of Cæsar

Hath too much mangled; whose repair and franchise

Shall, by the power we hold, be our good deed,

Though Rome be therefore angry. Mulmutius made our laws,

Who was the first of Britain which did put

His brows within a golden crown, and call'd

Himself a king.

LUCIUS.

I am sorry, Cymbeline,

That I am to pronounce Augustus Cæsar

(Cæsar, that hath moe kings his servants than

Thyself domestic officers) thine enemy.

Receive it from me, then: war and confusion

In Cæsar's name pronounce I 'gainst thee; look

For fury not to be resisted. Thus defied,

I thank thee for myself.

CYMBELINE.

Thou art welcome, Caius.

Thy Cæsar knighted me; my youth I spent

Much under him; of him I gather'd honour,

Which he to seek of me again, perforce,

Behoves me keep at utterance. I am perfect

That the Pannonians and Dalmatians for

Their liberties are now in arms, a precedent

Which not to read would show the Britons cold;

So Cæsar shall not find them.

LUCIUS.

Let proof speak.

CLOTEN.

His majesty bids you welcome. Make pastime with us a day or two, or longer. If you seek us afterwards in other terms, you shall find us in our salt-water girdle. If you beat us out of it, it is yours; if you fall in the adventure, our crows shall fare the better for you; and there's an end.

LUCIUS.

So, sir.

CYMBELINE.

I know your master's pleasure, and he mine;

All the remain is, welcome.

[Exeunt.]

SCENE II. Britain. Another room in Cymbeline's palace.

Enter Pisanio reading of a letter.

PISANIO.

How? of adultery? Wherefore write you not

What monsters her accuse? Leonatus!

O master, what a strange infection

Is fall'n into thy ear! What false Italian

(As poisonous-tongu'd as handed) hath prevail'd

On thy too ready hearing? Disloyal? No.

She's punish'd for her truth, and undergoes,

More goddess-like than wife-like, such assaults

As would take in some virtue. O my master,

Thy mind to her is now as low as were

Thy fortunes. How? that I should murder her?

Upon the love, and truth, and vows, which I

Have made to thy command? I, her? Her blood?

If it be so to do good service, never

Let me be counted serviceable. How look I

That I should seem to lack humanity

So much as this fact comes to?

[Reads.]

'Do't. The letter

That I have sent her, by her own command

Shall give thee opportunity.' O damn'd paper,

Black as the ink that's on thee! Senseless bauble,

Art thou a fedary for this act, and look'st

So virgin-like without? Lo, here she comes.

Enter Imogen.

I am ignorant in what I am commanded.

IMOGEN.

How now, Pisanio?

PISANIO.

Madam, here is a letter from my lord.

IMOGEN.

Who? thy lord? That is my lord, Leonatus?

O, learn'd indeed were that astronomer

That knew the stars as I his characters;

He'd lay the future open. You good gods,

Let what is here contain'd relish of love,

Of my lord's health, of his content; yet not

That we two are asunder; let that grieve him!

Some griefs are med'cinable; that is one of them,

For it doth physic love: of his content,

All but in that. Good wax, thy leave. Blest be

You bees that make these locks of counsel! Lovers

And men in dangerous bonds pray not alike;

Though forfeiters you cast in prison, yet

You clasp young Cupid's tables. Good news, gods!

[Reads.]

Justice and your father's wrath, should he take me in his dominion, could not be so cruel to me as you, O the dearest of creatures, would even renew me with your eyes. Take notice that I am in Cambria, at Milford Haven. What your own love will out of this advise you, follow. So he wishes you all happiness that remains loyal to his vow, and your increasing in love.

LEONATUS POSTHUMUS.

O for a horse with wings! Hear'st thou, Pisanio?

He is at Milford Haven. Read, and tell me

How far 'tis thither. If one of mean affairs

May plod it in a week, why may not I

Glide thither in a day? Then, true Pisanio,

Who long'st like me to see thy lord, who long'st

(O, let me 'bate!) but not like me, yet long'st,

But in a fainter kind. O, not like me,

For mine's beyond beyond: say, and speak thick,

(Love's counsellor should fill the bores of hearing

To th' smothering of the sense) how far it is

To this same blessed Milford. And by th' way

Tell me how Wales was made so happy as

T' inherit such a haven. But first of all,

How we may steal from hence; and for the gap

That we shall make in time from our hence-going

239

And our return, to excuse. But first, how get hence.

Why should excuse be born or ere begot?

We'll talk of that hereafter. Prithee speak,

How many score of miles may we well rid

'Twixt hour and hour?

PISANIO.

One score 'twixt sun and sun,

Madam, 's enough for you, and too much too.

IMOGEN.

Why, one that rode to's execution, man,

Could never go so slow. I have heard of riding wagers

Where horses have been nimbler than the sands

That run i' th' clock's behalf. But this is fool'ry.

Go bid my woman feign a sickness; say

She'll home to her father; and provide me presently

A riding suit, no costlier than would fit

A franklin's huswife.

PISANIO.

Madam, you're best consider.

IMOGEN.

I see before me, man. Nor here, nor here,

Nor what ensues, but have a fog in them

That I cannot look through. Away, I prithee;

Do as I bid thee. There's no more to say.

Accessible is none but Milford way.

[Exeunt.]

SCENE III. Wales. A mountainous country with a cave.

Enter from the cave Belarius, Guiderius and Arviragus.

BELARIUS.

A goodly day not to keep house with such

Whose roof's as low as ours! Stoop, boys; this gate

Instructs you how t' adore the heavens, and bows you

To a morning's holy office. The gates of monarchs

Are arch'd so high that giants may jet through

And keep their impious turbans on without

Good morrow to the sun. Hail, thou fair heaven!

We house i' th' rock, yet use thee not so hardly

As prouder livers do.

GUIDERIUS.

Hail, heaven!

ARVIRAGUS.

Hail, heaven!

BELARIUS.

Now for our mountain sport. Up to yond hill,

Your legs are young; I'll tread these flats. Consider,

When you above perceive me like a crow,

That it is place which lessens and sets off;

And you may then revolve what tales I have told you

Of courts, of princes, of the tricks in war.

This service is not service so being done,

But being so allow'd. To apprehend thus

Draws us a profit from all things we see,

And often to our comfort shall we find

The sharded beetle in a safer hold

Than is the full-wing'd eagle. O, this life

Is nobler than attending for a check,

Richer than doing nothing for a robe,

Prouder than rustling in unpaid-for silk:

Such gain the cap of him that makes him fine,

Yet keeps his book uncross'd. No life to ours!

GUIDERIUS.

Out of your proof you speak. We, poor unfledg'd,

Have never wing'd from view o' th' nest, nor know not

What air's from home. Haply this life is best,

If quiet life be best; sweeter to you

That have a sharper known; well corresponding

With your stiff age. But unto us it is

A cell of ignorance, travelling abed,

A prison for a debtor that not dares

To stride a limit.

ARVIRAGUS.

What should we speak of

When we are old as you? When we shall hear

The rain and wind beat dark December, how,

In this our pinching cave, shall we discourse.

The freezing hours away? We have seen nothing;

We are beastly: subtle as the fox for prey,

Like warlike as the wolf for what we eat.

Our valour is to chase what flies; our cage

We make a choir, as doth the prison'd bird,

And sing our bondage freely.

BELARIUS.

How you speak!

Did you but know the city's usuries,

And felt them knowingly; the art o' th' court,

As hard to leave as keep, whose top to climb

Is certain falling, or so slipp'ry that

The fear's as bad as falling; the toil o' th' war,

A pain that only seems to seek out danger

I' th' name of fame and honour, which dies i' th' search,

And hath as oft a sland'rous epitaph

As record of fair act; nay, many times,

Doth ill deserve by doing well; what's worse,

Must curtsy at the censure. O, boys, this story

The world may read in me; my body's mark'd

With Roman swords, and my report was once

First with the best of note. Cymbeline lov'd me;

And when a soldier was the theme, my name

Was not far off. Then was I as a tree

Whose boughs did bend with fruit. But in one night

A storm, or robbery, call it what you will,

Shook down my mellow hangings, nay, my leaves,

And left me bare to weather.

GUIDERIUS.

Uncertain favour!

BELARIUS.

My fault being nothing, as I have told you oft,

But that two villains, whose false oaths prevail'd

Before my perfect honour, swore to Cymbeline

I was confederate with the Romans. So

Follow'd my banishment, and this twenty years

This rock and these demesnes have been my world,

Where I have liv'd at honest freedom, paid

More pious debts to heaven than in all

The fore-end of my time. But up to th' mountains!

This is not hunters' language. He that strikes

The venison first shall be the lord o' th' feast;

To him the other two shall minister;

And we will fear no poison, which attends

In place of greater state. I'll meet you in the valleys.

       [Exeunt Guiderius and Arviragus.]

How hard it is to hide the sparks of nature!

These boys know little they are sons to th' King,

Nor Cymbeline dreams that they are alive.

They think they are mine; and though train'd up thus meanly

I' th' cave wherein they bow, their thoughts do hit

The roofs of palaces, and nature prompts them

In simple and low things to prince it much

Beyond the trick of others. This Polydore,

The heir of Cymbeline and Britain, who

The King his father call'd Guiderius—Jove!

When on my three-foot stool I sit and tell

The warlike feats I have done, his spirits fly out

Into my story; say 'Thus mine enemy fell,

And thus I set my foot on's neck'; even then

The princely blood flows in his cheek, he sweats,

Strains his young nerves, and puts himself in posture

That acts my words. The younger brother, Cadwal,

Once Arviragus, in as like a figure

Strikes life into my speech, and shows much more

His own conceiving. Hark, the game is rous'd!

O Cymbeline, heaven and my conscience knows

Thou didst unjustly banish me! Whereon,

At three and two years old, I stole these babes,

Thinking to bar thee of succession as

Thou refts me of my lands. Euriphile,

Thou wast their nurse; they took thee for their mother,

And every day do honour to her grave.

Myself, Belarius, that am Morgan call'd,

They take for natural father. The game is up.

[Exit.]

SCENE IV. Wales, near Milford Haven.

Enter Pisanio and Imogen.

IMOGEN.

Thou told'st me, when we came from horse, the place

Was near at hand. Ne'er long'd my mother so

To see me first as I have now. Pisanio! Man!

Where is Posthumus? What is in thy mind

That makes thee stare thus? Wherefore breaks that sigh

From th' inward of thee? One but painted thus

Would be interpreted a thing perplex'd

Beyond self-explication. Put thyself

Into a haviour of less fear, ere wildness

Vanquish my staider senses. What's the matter?

Why tender'st thou that paper to me with

A look untender? If't be summer news,

Smile to't before; if winterly, thou need'st

But keep that count'nance still. My husband's hand?

That drug-damn'd Italy hath out-crafted him,

And he's at some hard point. Speak, man; thy tongue

May take off some extremity, which to read

Would be even mortal to me.

PISANIO.

Please you read,

And you shall find me, wretched man, a thing

The most disdain'd of fortune.

IMOGEN.

[Reads.] Thy mistress, Pisanio, hath play'd the strumpet in my bed, the testimonies whereof lie bleeding in me. I speak not out of weak surmises, but from proof as strong as my grief and as certain as I expect my revenge. That part thou, Pisanio, must act for me, if thy faith be not tainted with the breach of hers. Let thine own hands take away her life; I shall give thee opportunity at Milford Haven; she hath my letter for the purpose; where, if thou fear to strike, and to make me certain it is done, thou art the pandar to her dishonour, and equally to me disloyal.

PISANIO.

What shall I need to draw my sword? The paper

Hath cut her throat already. No, 'tis slander,

Whose edge is sharper than the sword, whose tongue

Outvenoms all the worms of Nile, whose breath

Rides on the posting winds and doth belie

All corners of the world. Kings, queens, and states,

Maids, matrons, nay, the secrets of the grave,

This viperous slander enters. What cheer, madam?

IMOGEN.

False to his bed? What is it to be false?

To lie in watch there, and to think on him?

To weep twixt clock and clock? If sleep charge nature,

To break it with a fearful dream of him,

And cry myself awake? That's false to's bed,

Is it?

PISANIO.

Alas, good lady!

IMOGEN.

I false! Thy conscience witness! Iachimo,

Thou didst accuse him of incontinency;

Thou then look'dst like a villain; now, methinks,

Thy favour's good enough. Some jay of Italy,

Whose mother was her painting, hath betray'd him.

Poor I am stale, a garment out of fashion,

And for I am richer than to hang by th' walls

I must be ripp'd. To pieces with me! O,

Men's vows are women's traitors! All good seeming,

By thy revolt, O husband, shall be thought

Put on for villainy; not born where't grows,

But worn a bait for ladies.

PISANIO.

Good madam, hear me.

IMOGEN.

True honest men being heard, like false Æneas,

Were, in his time, thought false; and Sinon's weeping

Did scandal many a holy tear, took pity

From most true wretchedness. So thou, Posthumus,

Wilt lay the leaven on all proper men:

Goodly and gallant shall be false and perjur'd

From thy great fail. Come, fellow, be thou honest;

Do thou thy master's bidding; when thou seest him,

A little witness my obedience. Look!

I draw the sword myself; take it, and hit

The innocent mansion of my love, my heart.

Fear not; 'tis empty of all things but grief;

Thy master is not there, who was indeed

The riches of it. Do his bidding; strike.

Thou mayst be valiant in a better cause,

But now thou seem'st a coward.

PISANIO.

Hence, vile instrument!

Thou shalt not damn my hand.

IMOGEN.

Why, I must die;

And if I do not by thy hand, thou art

No servant of thy master's. Against self-slaughter

There is a prohibition so divine

That cravens my weak hand. Come, here's my heart:

Something's afore't. Soft, soft! we'll no defence,

Obedient as the scabbard. What is here?

The scriptures of the loyal Leonatus

All turn'd to heresy? Away, away,

Corrupters of my faith, you shall no more

Be stomachers to my heart. Thus may poor fools

Believe false teachers; though those that are betray'd

Do feel the treason sharply, yet the traitor

Stands in worse case of woe. And thou, Posthumus,

That didst set up my disobedience 'gainst the King

My father, and make me put into contempt the suits

Of princely fellows, shalt hereafter find

It is no act of common passage but

A strain of rareness; and I grieve myself

To think, when thou shalt be disedg'd by her

That now thou tirest on, how thy memory

Will then be pang'd by me. Prithee dispatch.

The lamp entreats the butcher. Where's thy knife?

Thou art too slow to do thy master's bidding,

When I desire it too.

PISANIO.

O gracious lady,

Since I receiv'd command to do this busines

I have not slept one wink.

IMOGEN.

Do't, and to bed then.

PISANIO.

I'll wake mine eyeballs first.

IMOGEN.

Wherefore then

Didst undertake it? Why hast thou abus'd

So many miles with a pretence? This place?

Mine action and thine own? our horses' labour?

The time inviting thee? The perturb'd court,

For my being absent? whereunto I never

Purpose return. Why hast thou gone so far

To be unbent when thou hast ta'en thy stand,

Th' elected deer before thee?

PISANIO.

But to win time

To lose so bad employment, in the which

I have consider'd of a course. Good lady,

Hear me with patience.

IMOGEN.

Talk thy tongue weary, speak.

I have heard I am a strumpet, and mine ear,

Therein false struck, can take no greater wound,

Nor tent to bottom that. But speak.

PISANIO.

Then, madam,

I thought you would not back again.

IMOGEN.

Most like,

Bringing me here to kill me.

PISANIO.

Not so, neither;

But if I were as wise as honest, then

My purpose would prove well. It cannot be

But that my master is abus'd. Some villain,

Ay, and singular in his art, hath done you both

This cursed injury.

IMOGEN.

Some Roman courtezan!

PISANIO.

No, on my life!

I'll give but notice you are dead, and send him

Some bloody sign of it, for 'tis commanded

I should do so. You shall be miss'd at court,

And that will well confirm it.

IMOGEN.

Why, good fellow,

What shall I do the while? Where bide? How live?

Or in my life what comfort, when I am

Dead to my husband?

PISANIO.

If you'll back to th' court—

IMOGEN.

No court, no father, nor no more ado

With that harsh, noble, simple nothing,

That Cloten, whose love-suit hath been to me

As fearful as a siege.

PISANIO.

If not at court,

Then not in Britain must you bide.

IMOGEN.

Where then?

Hath Britain all the sun that shines? Day, night,

Are they not but in Britain? I' th' world's volume

Our Britain seems as of it, but not in't;

In a great pool a swan's nest. Prithee think

There's livers out of Britain.

PISANIO.

I am most glad

You think of other place. Th' ambassador,

Lucius the Roman, comes to Milford Haven

Tomorrow. Now, if you could wear a mind

Dark as your fortune is, and but disguise

That which t' appear itself must not yet be

But by self-danger, you should tread a course

Pretty and full of view; yea, happily, near

The residence of Posthumus; so nigh, at least,

That though his actions were not visible, yet

Report should render him hourly to your ear

As truly as he moves.

IMOGEN.

O! for such means,

Though peril to my modesty, not death on't,

I would adventure.

PISANIO.

Well then, here's the point:

You must forget to be a woman; change

Command into obedience; fear and niceness

(The handmaids of all women, or, more truly,

Woman it pretty self) into a waggish courage;

Ready in gibes, quick-answer'd, saucy, and

As quarrelous as the weasel. Nay, you must

Forget that rarest treasure of your cheek,

Exposing it (but, O, the harder heart!

Alack, no remedy) to the greedy touch

Of common-kissing Titan, and forget

Your laboursome and dainty trims wherein

You made great Juno angry.

IMOGEN.

Nay, be brief;

I see into thy end, and am almost

A man already.

PISANIO.

First, make yourself but like one.

Fore-thinking this, I have already fit

('Tis in my cloak-bag) doublet, hat, hose, all

That answer to them. Would you, in their serving,

And with what imitation you can borrow

From youth of such a season, 'fore noble Lucius

Present yourself, desire his service, tell him

Wherein you're happy; which will make him know

If that his head have ear in music; doubtless

With joy he will embrace you; for he's honourable,

And, doubling that, most holy. Your means abroad:

You have me, rich; and I will never fail

Beginning nor supplyment.

IMOGEN.

Thou art all the comfort

The gods will diet me with. Prithee away!

There's more to be consider'd; but we'll even

All that good time will give us. This attempt

I am soldier to, and will abide it with

A prince's courage. Away, I prithee.

PISANIO.

Well, madam, we must take a short farewell,

Lest, being miss'd, I be suspected of

Your carriage from the court. My noble mistress,

Here is a box; I had it from the Queen.

What's in't is precious. If you are sick at sea

Or stomach-qualm'd at land, a dram of this

Will drive away distemper. To some shade,

And fit you to your manhood. May the gods

Direct you to the best!

IMOGEN.

Amen. I thank thee.

[Exeunt severally.]

SCENE V. Britain. Cymbeline's palace.

Enter Cymbeline, Queen, Cloten, Lucius and Lords.

CYMBELINE.

Thus far, and so farewell.

LUCIUS.

Thanks, royal sir.

My emperor hath wrote; I must from hence,

And am right sorry that I must report ye

My master's enemy.

CYMBELINE.

Our subjects, sir,

Will not endure his yoke; and for ourself

To show less sovereignty than they, must needs

Appear unkinglike.

LUCIUS.

So, sir. I desire of you

A conduct overland to Milford Haven.

Madam, all joy befall your Grace, and you!

CYMBELINE.

My lords, you are appointed for that office;

The due of honour in no point omit.

So farewell, noble Lucius.

LUCIUS.

Your hand, my lord.

CLOTEN.

Receive it friendly; but from this time forth

I wear it as your enemy.

LUCIUS.

Sir, the event

Is yet to name the winner. Fare you well.

CYMBELINE.

Leave not the worthy Lucius, good my lords,

Till he have cross'd the Severn. Happiness!

[Exeunt Lucius and Lords.]

QUEEN.

He goes hence frowning; but it honours us

That we have given him cause.

CLOTEN.

'Tis all the better;

Your valiant Britons have their wishes in it.

CYMBELINE.

Lucius hath wrote already to the Emperor

How it goes here. It fits us therefore ripely

Our chariots and our horsemen be in readiness.

The pow'rs that he already hath in Gallia

Will soon be drawn to head, from whence he moves

His war for Britain.

QUEEN.

'Tis not sleepy business,

But must be look'd to speedily and strongly.

CYMBELINE.

Our expectation that it would be thus

Hath made us forward. But, my gentle queen,

Where is our daughter? She hath not appear'd

Before the Roman, nor to us hath tender'd

The duty of the day. She looks us like

A thing more made of malice than of duty;

We have noted it. Call her before us, for

We have been too slight in sufferance.

[Exit an Attendant.]

QUEEN.

Royal sir,

Since the exile of Posthumus, most retir'd

Hath her life been; the cure whereof, my lord,

'Tis time must do. Beseech your Majesty,

Forbear sharp speeches to her; she's a lady

So tender of rebukes that words are strokes,

And strokes death to her.

Enter Attendant.

CYMBELINE.

Where is she, sir? How

Can her contempt be answer'd?

ATTENDANT.

Please you, sir,

Her chambers are all lock'd, and there's no answer

That will be given to th' loud of noise we make.

QUEEN.

My lord, when last I went to visit her,

She pray'd me to excuse her keeping close;

Whereto constrain'd by her infirmity

She should that duty leave unpaid to you

Which daily she was bound to proffer. This

She wish'd me to make known; but our great court

Made me to blame in memory.

CYMBELINE.

Her doors lock'd?

Not seen of late? Grant, heavens, that which I fear

Prove false!

[Exit.]

QUEEN.

Son, I say, follow the King.

CLOTEN.

That man of hers, Pisanio, her old servant,

I have not seen these two days.

QUEEN.

Go, look after.

[Exit Cloten.]

Pisanio, thou that stand'st so for Posthumus!

He hath a drug of mine. I pray his absence

Proceed by swallowing that; for he believes

It is a thing most precious. But for her,

Where is she gone? Haply despair hath seiz'd her;

Or, wing'd with fervour of her love, she's flown

To her desir'd Posthumus. Gone she is

To death or to dishonour, and my end

Can make good use of either. She being down,

I have the placing of the British crown.

Enter Cloten.

How now, my son?

CLOTEN.

'Tis certain she is fled.

Go in and cheer the King. He rages; none

Dare come about him.

QUEEN.

All the better. May

This night forestall him of the coming day!

[Exit.]

CLOTEN.

I love and hate her; for she's fair and royal,

And that she hath all courtly parts more exquisite

Than lady, ladies, woman. From every one

The best she hath, and she, of all compounded,

Outsells them all. I love her therefore; but

Disdaining me and throwing favours on

The low Posthumus slanders so her judgement

That what's else rare is chok'd; and in that point

I will conclude to hate her, nay, indeed,

To be reveng'd upon her. For when fools

Shall—

Enter Pisanio.

Who is here? What, are you packing, sirrah?

Come hither. Ah, you precious pandar! Villain,

Where is thy lady? In a word, or else

Thou art straightway with the fiends.

PISANIO.

O good my lord!

CLOTEN.

Where is thy lady? or, by Jupiter—

I will not ask again. Close villain,

I'll have this secret from thy heart, or rip

Thy heart to find it. Is she with Posthumus?

From whose so many weights of baseness cannot

A dram of worth be drawn.

PISANIO.

Alas, my lord,

How can she be with him? When was she miss'd?

He is in Rome.

CLOTEN.

Where is she, sir? Come nearer.

No farther halting! Satisfy me home

What is become of her.

PISANIO.

O my all-worthy lord!

CLOTEN.

All-worthy villain!

Discover where thy mistress is at once,

At the next word. No more of 'worthy lord'!

Speak, or thy silence on the instant is

Thy condemnation and thy death.

PISANIO.

Then, sir,

This paper is the history of my knowledge

Touching her flight.

[Presenting a letter.]

CLOTEN.

Let's see't. I will pursue her

Even to Augustus' throne.

PISANIO.

[Aside.] Or this or perish.

She's far enough; and what he learns by this

May prove his travel, not her danger.

CLOTEN.

Humh!

PISANIO.

[Aside.] I'll write to my lord she's dead. O Imogen,

Safe mayst thou wander, safe return again!

CLOTEN.

Sirrah, is this letter true?

PISANIO.

Sir, as I think.

CLOTEN.

It is Posthumus' hand; I know't. Sirrah, if thou wouldst not be a villain, but do me true service, undergo those employments wherein I should have cause to use thee with a serious industry—that is, what villainy soe'er I bid thee do, to perform it directly and truly—I would think thee an honest man; thou shouldst neither want my means for thy relief nor my voice for thy preferment.

PISANIO.

Well, my good lord.

CLOTEN.

Wilt thou serve me? For since patiently and constantly thou hast stuck to the bare fortune of that beggar Posthumus, thou canst not, in the course of gratitude, but be a diligent follower of mine. Wilt thou serve me?

PISANIO.

Sir, I will.

CLOTEN.

Give me thy hand; here's my purse. Hast any of thy late master's garments in thy possession?

PISANIO.

I have, my lord, at my lodging, the same suit he wore when he took leave of my lady and mistress.

CLOTEN.

The first service thou dost me, fetch that suit hither. Let it be thy first service; go.

PISANIO.

I shall, my lord.

[Exit.]

CLOTEN.

Meet thee at Milford Haven! I forgot to ask him one thing; I'll remember't anon. Even there, thou villain Posthumus, will I kill thee. I would these garments were come. She said upon a time—the bitterness of it I now belch from my heart—that she held the very garment of Posthumus in more respect than my noble and natural person, together with the adornment of my qualities. With that suit upon my back will I ravish her; first kill him, and in her eyes. There shall she see my valour, which will then be a torment to her contempt. He on the ground, my speech of insultment ended on his dead body, and when my lust hath dined—which, as I say, to vex her I will execute in the clothes that she so prais'd—to the court I'll knock her back, foot her home again. She hath despis'd me rejoicingly, and I'll be merry in my revenge.

Enter Pisanio with the clothes.

Be those the garments?

PISANIO.

Ay, my noble lord.

CLOTEN.

How long is't since she went to Milford Haven?

PISANIO.

She can scarce be there yet.

CLOTEN.

Bring this apparel to my chamber; that is the second thing that I have commanded thee. The third is that thou wilt be a voluntary mute to my design. Be but duteous and true, preferment shall tender itself to thee. My revenge is now at Milford, would I had wings to follow it! Come, and be true.

[Exit.]

PISANIO.

Thou bid'st me to my loss; for true to thee

Were to prove false, which I will never be,

To him that is most true. To Milford go,

And find not her whom thou pursuest. Flow, flow,

You heavenly blessings, on her! This fool's speed

Be cross'd with slowness! Labour be his meed!

[Exit.]

SCENE VI. Wales. Before the cave of Belarius.

Enter Imogen alone, in boy's clothes.

IMOGEN.

I see a man's life is a tedious one.

I have tir'd myself, and for two nights together

Have made the ground my bed. I should be sick

But that my resolution helps me. Milford,

When from the mountain-top Pisanio show'd thee,

Thou wast within a ken. O Jove! I think

Foundations fly the wretched; such, I mean,

Where they should be reliev'd. Two beggars told me

I could not miss my way. Will poor folks lie,

That have afflictions on them, knowing 'tis

A punishment or trial? Yes; no wonder,

When rich ones scarce tell true. To lapse in fulness

Is sorer than to lie for need; and falsehood

Is worse in kings than beggars. My dear lord!

Thou art one o' th' false ones. Now I think on thee

My hunger's gone; but even before, I was

At point to sink for food. But what is this?

Here is a path to't; 'tis some savage hold.

I were best not call; I dare not call. Yet famine,

Ere clean it o'erthrow nature, makes it valiant.

Plenty and peace breeds cowards; hardness ever

Of hardiness is mother. Ho! who's here?

If anything that's civil, speak; if savage,

Take or lend. Ho! No answer? Then I'll enter.

Best draw my sword; and if mine enemy

But fear the sword, like me, he'll scarcely look on't.

Such a foe, good heavens!

[Exit into the cave.]

SCENE VII. The same.

Enter Belarius, Guiderius and Arviragus.

BELARIUS.

You, Polydore, have prov'd best woodman and

Are master of the feast. Cadwal and I

Will play the cook and servant; 'tis our match.

The sweat of industry would dry and die

But for the end it works to. Come, our stomachs

Will make what's homely savoury; weariness

Can snore upon the flint, when resty sloth

Finds the down pillow hard. Now, peace be here,

Poor house, that keep'st thyself!

GUIDERIUS.

I am thoroughly weary.

ARVIRAGUS.

I am weak with toil, yet strong in appetite.

GUIDERIUS.

There is cold meat i' th' cave; we'll browse on that

Whilst what we have kill'd be cook'd.

BELARIUS.

[Looking into the cave.] Stay, come not in.

But that it eats our victuals, I should think

Here were a fairy.

GUIDERIUS.

What's the matter, sir?

BELARIUS.

By Jupiter, an angel! or, if not,

An earthly paragon! Behold divineness

No elder than a boy!

Enter Imogen.

IMOGEN.

Good masters, harm me not.

Before I enter'd here I call'd, and thought

To have begg'd or bought what I have took. Good troth,

I have stol'n nought; nor would not though I had found

Gold strew'd i' th' floor. Here's money for my meat.

I would have left it on the board, so soon

As I had made my meal, and parted

With pray'rs for the provider.

GUIDERIUS.

Money, youth?

ARVIRAGUS.

All gold and silver rather turn to dirt,

As 'tis no better reckon'd but of those

Who worship dirty gods.

IMOGEN.

272

I see you're angry.

Know, if you kill me for my fault, I should

Have died had I not made it.

BELARIUS.

Whither bound?

IMOGEN.

To Milford Haven.

BELARIUS.

What's your name?

IMOGEN.

Fidele, sir. I have a kinsman who

Is bound for Italy; he embark'd at Milford;

To whom being going, almost spent with hunger,

I am fall'n in this offence.

BELARIUS.

Prithee, fair youth,

Think us no churls, nor measure our good minds

By this rude place we live in. Well encounter'd!

'Tis almost night; you shall have better cheer

Ere you depart, and thanks to stay and eat it.

Boys, bid him welcome.

GUIDERIUS.

Were you a woman, youth,

I should woo hard but be your groom. In honesty

I bid for you as I'd buy.

ARVIRAGUS.

I'll make't my comfort

He is a man. I'll love him as my brother;

And such a welcome as I'd give to him

After long absence, such is yours. Most welcome!

Be sprightly, for you fall 'mongst friends.

IMOGEN.

'Mongst friends,

If brothers. [Aside.] Would it had been so that they

Had been my father's sons! Then had my prize

Been less, and so more equal ballasting

To thee, Posthumus.

BELARIUS.

He wrings at some distress.

GUIDERIUS.

Would I could free't!

ARVIRAGUS.

Or I, whate'er it be,

What pain it cost, what danger! Gods!

BELARIUS.

[Whispering.] Hark, boys.

IMOGEN.

274

[Aside.] Great men,

That had a court no bigger than this cave,

That did attend themselves, and had the virtue

Which their own conscience seal'd them, laying by

That nothing-gift of differing multitudes,

Could not out-peer these twain. Pardon me, gods!

I'd change my sex to be companion with them,

Since Leonatus false.

BELARIUS.

It shall be so.

Boys, we'll go dress our hunt. Fair youth, come in.

Discourse is heavy, fasting; when we have supp'd,

We'll mannerly demand thee of thy story,

So far as thou wilt speak it.

GUIDERIUS.

Pray draw near.

ARVIRAGUS.

The night to th' owl and morn to th' lark less

welcome.

IMOGEN.

Thanks, sir.

ARVIRAGUS.

I pray draw near.

[Exeunt.]

275

SCENE VIII. Rome. A public place.

Enter two Roman Senators and Tribunes.

FIRST SENATOR.

This is the tenour of the Emperor's writ:

That since the common men are now in action

'Gainst the Pannonians and Dalmatians,

And that the legions now in Gallia are

Full weak to undertake our wars against

The fall'n-off Britons, that we do incite

The gentry to this business. He creates

Lucius proconsul; and to you, the tribunes,

For this immediate levy, he commands

His absolute commission. Long live Cæsar!

TRIBUNE.

Is Lucius general of the forces?

SECOND SENATOR.

Ay.

TRIBUNE.

Remaining now in Gallia?

FIRST SENATOR.

With those legions

Which I have spoke of, whereunto your levy

Must be supplyant. The words of your commission

Will tie you to the numbers and the time

Of their dispatch.

TRIBUNE.

We will discharge our duty.

[Exeunt.]

ACT IV

SCENE I. Wales. Near the cave of Belarius.

Enter Cloten alone.

CLOTEN.

I am near to th' place where they should meet, if Pisanio have mapp'd it truly. How fit his garments serve me! Why should his mistress, who was made by him that made the tailor, not be fit too? The rather, saving reverence of the word, for 'tis said a woman's fitness comes by fits. Therein I must play the workman. I dare speak it to myself, for it is not vain-glory for a man and his glass to confer in his own chamber; I mean, the lines of my body are as well drawn as his; no less young, more strong, not beneath him in fortunes, beyond him in the advantage of the time, above him in birth, alike conversant in general services, and more remarkable in single oppositions. Yet this imperceiverant thing loves him in my despite. What mortality is! Posthumus, thy head, which now is growing upon thy shoulders, shall within this hour be off; thy mistress enforced; thy garments cut to pieces before her face; and all this done, spurn her home to her father, who may, haply, be a little angry for my so rough usage; but my mother, having power of his testiness, shall turn all into my commendations. My horse is tied up safe. Out, sword, and to a sore purpose! Fortune, put them into my hand. This is the very description of their meeting-place; and the fellow dares not deceive me.

[Exit.]

SCENE II. Wales. Before the cave of Belarius.

Enter from the cave, Belarius, Guiderius, Arviragus and Imogen.

BELARIUS.

[To Imogen.] You are not well. Remain here in the cave;

We'll come to you after hunting.

ARVIRAGUS.

[To Imogen.] Brother, stay here.

Are we not brothers?

IMOGEN.

So man and man should be;

But clay and clay differs in dignity,

Whose dust is both alike. I am very sick.

GUIDERIUS.

Go you to hunting; I'll abide with him.

IMOGEN.

So sick I am not, yet I am not well;

But not so citizen a wanton as

To seem to die ere sick. So please you, leave me;

Stick to your journal course. The breach of custom

Is breach of all. I am ill, but your being by me

Cannot amend me; society is no comfort

To one not sociable. I am not very sick,

Since I can reason of it. Pray you trust me here.

I'll rob none but myself; and let me die,

Stealing so poorly.

GUIDERIUS.

I love thee; I have spoke it.

How much the quantity, the weight as much

As I do love my father.

BELARIUS.

What? how? how?

ARVIRAGUS.

If it be sin to say so, sir, I yoke me

In my good brother's fault. I know not why

I love this youth, and I have heard you say

Love's reason's without reason. The bier at door,

And a demand who is't shall die, I'd say

'My father, not this youth.'

BELARIUS.

[Aside.] O noble strain!

O worthiness of nature! breed of greatness!

Cowards father cowards and base things sire base.

Nature hath meal and bran, contempt and grace.

I'm not their father; yet who this should be

Doth miracle itself, lov'd before me.—

'Tis the ninth hour o' th' morn.

ARVIRAGUS.

Brother, farewell.

IMOGEN.

I wish ye sport.

ARVIRAGUS.

Your health. [To Belarius.] So please you, sir.

IMOGEN.

[Aside.] These are kind creatures. Gods, what lies I

have heard!

Our courtiers say all's savage but at court.

Experience, O, thou disprov'st report!

Th' imperious seas breed monsters; for the dish,

Poor tributary rivers as sweet fish.

I am sick still; heart-sick. Pisanio,

I'll now taste of thy drug.

[Swallows some.]

GUIDERIUS.

I could not stir him.

He said he was gentle, but unfortunate;

Dishonestly afflicted, but yet honest.

ARVIRAGUS.

Thus did he answer me; yet said hereafter

I might know more.

BELARIUS.

To th' field, to th' field!

We'll leave you for this time. Go in and rest.

ARVIRAGUS.

We'll not be long away.

BELARIUS.

Pray be not sick,

For you must be our huswife.

IMOGEN.

Well, or ill,

I am bound to you.

BELARIUS.

And shalt be ever.

[Exit Imogen into the cave.]

This youth, howe'er distress'd, appears he hath had

Good ancestors.

ARVIRAGUS.

How angel-like he sings!

GUIDERIUS.

But his neat cookery! He cut our roots in characters,

And sauc'd our broths as Juno had been sick,

And he her dieter.

ARVIRAGUS.

Nobly he yokes

A smiling with a sigh, as if the sigh

Was that it was for not being such a smile;

The smile mocking the sigh that it would fly

From so divine a temple to commix

With winds that sailors rail at.

GUIDERIUS.

I do note

That grief and patience, rooted in him both,

Mingle their spurs together.

ARVIRAGUS.

Grow patience!

And let the stinking elder, grief, untwine

His perishing root with the increasing vine!

BELARIUS.

It is great morning. Come, away! Who's there?

Enter Cloten.

CLOTEN.

I cannot find those runagates; that villain

Hath mock'd me. I am faint.

BELARIUS.

Those runagates?

Means he not us? I partly know him; 'tis

Cloten, the son o' th' Queen. I fear some ambush.

I saw him not these many years, and yet

I know 'tis he. We are held as outlaws. Hence!

GUIDERIUS.

He is but one; you and my brother search

What companies are near. Pray you away;

Let me alone with him.

[Exeunt Belarius and Arviragus.]

CLOTEN.

Soft! What are you

That fly me thus? Some villain mountaineers?

I have heard of such. What slave art thou?

GUIDERIUS.

A thing

More slavish did I ne'er than answering

A slave without a knock.

CLOTEN.

Thou art a robber,

A law-breaker, a villain. Yield thee, thief.

GUIDERIUS.

To who? To thee? What art thou? Have not I

An arm as big as thine, a heart as big?

Thy words, I grant, are bigger, for I wear not

My dagger in my mouth. Say what thou art;

Why I should yield to thee.

CLOTEN.

Thou villain base,

Know'st me not by my clothes?

GUIDERIUS.

No, nor thy tailor, rascal,

Who is thy grandfather; he made those clothes,

Which, as it seems, make thee.

CLOTEN.

Thou precious varlet,

My tailor made them not.

GUIDERIUS.

Hence, then, and thank

The man that gave them thee. Thou art some fool;

I am loath to beat thee.

CLOTEN.

Thou injurious thief,

Hear but my name, and tremble.

GUIDERIUS.

What's thy name?

CLOTEN.

Cloten, thou villain.

GUIDERIUS.

Cloten, thou double villain, be thy name,

I cannot tremble at it. Were it Toad, or Adder, Spider,

'Twould move me sooner.

CLOTEN.

To thy further fear,

Nay, to thy mere confusion, thou shalt know

I am son to th' Queen.

GUIDERIUS.

I'm sorry for't; not seeming

So worthy as thy birth.

CLOTEN.

Art not afeard?

GUIDERIUS.

Those that I reverence, those I fear—the wise;

At fools I laugh, not fear them.

CLOTEN.

Die the death.

When I have slain thee with my proper hand,

I'll follow those that even now fled hence,

And on the gates of Lud's Town set your heads.

Yield, rustic mountaineer.

[Exeunt, fighting.]

Enter Belarius and Arviragus.

BELARIUS.

No company's abroad?

ARVIRAGUS.

None in the world; you did mistake him, sure.

BELARIUS.

I cannot tell; long is it since I saw him,

But time hath nothing blurr'd those lines of favour

Which then he wore; the snatches in his voice,

And burst of speaking, were as his. I am absolute

'Twas very Cloten.

ARVIRAGUS.

In this place we left them.

I wish my brother make good time with him,

You say he is so fell.

BELARIUS.

Being scarce made up,

I mean to man, he had not apprehension

Or roaring terrors; for defect of judgement

Is oft the cease of fear.

Enter Guiderius with Cloten's head.

But, see, thy brother.

GUIDERIUS.

This Cloten was a fool, an empty purse;

There was no money in't. Not Hercules

Could have knock'd out his brains, for he had none;

Yet I not doing this, the fool had borne

My head as I do his.

BELARIUS.

What hast thou done?

GUIDERIUS.

I am perfect what: cut off one Cloten's head,

Son to the Queen, after his own report;

Who call'd me traitor, mountaineer, and swore

With his own single hand he'd take us in,

Displace our heads where, thank the gods, they grow,

And set them on Lud's Town.

BELARIUS.

We are all undone.

GUIDERIUS.

Why, worthy father, what have we to lose

But that he swore to take, our lives? The law

Protects not us; then why should we be tender

To let an arrogant piece of flesh threat us,

Play judge and executioner all himself,

For we do fear the law? What company

Discover you abroad?

BELARIUS.

No single soul

Can we set eye on, but in all safe reason

He must have some attendants. Though his humour

Was nothing but mutation, ay, and that

From one bad thing to worse, not frenzy, not

Absolute madness could so far have rav'd,

To bring him here alone. Although perhaps

It may be heard at court that such as we

Cave here, hunt here, are outlaws, and in time

May make some stronger head, the which he hearing,

As it is like him, might break out and swear

He'd fetch us in; yet is't not probable

To come alone, either he so undertaking

Or they so suffering. Then on good ground we fear,

If we do fear this body hath a tail

More perilous than the head.

ARVIRAGUS.

Let ordinance

Come as the gods foresay it. Howsoe'er,

My brother hath done well.

BELARIUS.

I had no mind

To hunt this day; the boy Fidele's sickness

Did make my way long forth.

GUIDERIUS.

With his own sword,

Which he did wave against my throat, I have ta'en

His head from him. I'll throw't into the creek

Behind our rock, and let it to the sea

And tell the fishes he's the Queen's son, Cloten.

That's all I reck.

[Exit.]

BELARIUS.

I fear 'twill be reveng'd.

Would, Polydore, thou hadst not done't! though valour

Becomes thee well enough.

ARVIRAGUS.

Would I had done't,

So the revenge alone pursu'd me! Polydore,

I love thee brotherly, but envy much

Thou hast robb'd me of this deed. I would revenges,

That possible strength might meet, would seek us through,

And put us to our answer.

BELARIUS.

Well, 'tis done.

We'll hunt no more today, nor seek for danger

Where there's no profit. I prithee to our rock.

You and Fidele play the cooks; I'll stay

Till hasty Polydore return, and bring him

To dinner presently.

ARVIRAGUS.

Poor sick Fidele!

I'll willingly to him; to gain his colour

I'd let a parish of such Cloten's blood,

And praise myself for charity.

[Exit.]

BELARIUS.

O thou goddess,

Thou divine Nature, thou thyself thou blazon'st

In these two princely boys! They are as gentle

As zephyrs blowing below the violet,

Not wagging his sweet head; and yet as rough,

Their royal blood enchaf'd, as the rud'st wind

That by the top doth take the mountain pine

And make him stoop to th' vale. 'Tis wonder

That an invisible instinct should frame them

To royalty unlearn'd, honour untaught,

Civility not seen from other, valour

That wildly grows in them, but yields a crop

As if it had been sow'd. Yet still it's strange

What Cloten's being here to us portends,

Or what his death will bring us.

Enter Guiderius.

GUIDERIUS.

Where's my brother?

I have sent Cloten's clotpoll down the stream,

In embassy to his mother; his body's hostage

For his return.

[Solemn music.]

BELARIUS.

My ingenious instrument!

Hark, Polydore, it sounds. But what occasion

Hath Cadwal now to give it motion? Hark!

GUIDERIUS.

Is he at home?

BELARIUS.

He went hence even now.

GUIDERIUS.

What does he mean? Since death of my dear'st mother

It did not speak before. All solemn things

Should answer solemn accidents. The matter?

Triumphs for nothing and lamenting toys

Is jollity for apes and grief for boys.

Is Cadwal mad?

Enter Arviragus with Imogen as dead, bearing her in his arms.

BELARIUS.

Look, here he comes,

And brings the dire occasion in his arms

Of what we blame him for!

ARVIRAGUS.

The bird is dead

That we have made so much on. I had rather

Have skipp'd from sixteen years of age to sixty,

To have turn'd my leaping time into a crutch,

Than have seen this.

GUIDERIUS.

O sweetest, fairest lily!

My brother wears thee not the one half so well

As when thou grew'st thyself.

BELARIUS.

O melancholy!

Who ever yet could sound thy bottom? find

The ooze to show what coast thy sluggish crare

Might'st easiliest harbour in? Thou blessed thing!

Jove knows what man thou mightst have made; but I,

Thou diedst, a most rare boy, of melancholy.

How found you him?

ARVIRAGUS.

Stark, as you see;

Thus smiling, as some fly had tickled slumber,

Not as death's dart, being laugh'd at; his right cheek

Reposing on a cushion.

GUIDERIUS.

Where?

ARVIRAGUS.

O' th' floor;

His arms thus leagu'd. I thought he slept, and put

My clouted brogues from off my feet, whose rudeness

Answer'd my steps too loud.

GUIDERIUS.

Why, he but sleeps.

If he be gone he'll make his grave a bed;

With female fairies will his tomb be haunted,

And worms will not come to thee.

ARVIRAGUS.

With fairest flowers,

Whilst summer lasts and I live here, Fidele,

I'll sweeten thy sad grave. Thou shalt not lack

The flower that's like thy face, pale primrose; nor

The azur'd hare-bell, like thy veins; no, nor

The leaf of eglantine, whom not to slander,

Out-sweet'ned not thy breath. The ruddock would,

With charitable bill (O bill, sore shaming

Those rich-left heirs that let their fathers lie

Without a monument!) bring thee all this;

Yea, and furr'd moss besides, when flow'rs are none,

To winter-ground thy corse—

GUIDERIUS.

Prithee have done,

And do not play in wench-like words with that

Which is so serious. Let us bury him,

And not protract with admiration what

Is now due debt. To th' grave.

ARVIRAGUS.

Say, where shall's lay him?

GUIDERIUS.

By good Euriphile, our mother.

ARVIRAGUS.

Be't so;

And let us, Polydore, though now our voices

Have got the mannish crack, sing him to th' ground,

As once to our mother; use like note and words,

Save that Euriphile must be Fidele.

GUIDERIUS.

Cadwal,

I cannot sing. I'll weep, and word it with thee;

For notes of sorrow out of tune are worse

Than priests and fanes that lie.

ARVIRAGUS.

We'll speak it, then.

BELARIUS.

Great griefs, I see, med'cine the less, for Cloten

Is quite forgot. He was a queen's son, boys;

And though he came our enemy, remember

He was paid for that. Though mean and mighty rotting

Together have one dust, yet reverence,

That angel of the world, doth make distinction

Of place 'tween high and low. Our foe was princely;

And though you took his life, as being our foe,

Yet bury him as a prince.

GUIDERIUS.

Pray you fetch him hither.

Thersites' body is as good as Ajax',

When neither are alive.

ARVIRAGUS.

If you'll go fetch him,

We'll say our song the whilst. Brother, begin.

[Exit Belarius.]

GUIDERIUS.

Nay, Cadwal, we must lay his head to th' East;

My father hath a reason for't.

ARVIRAGUS.

'Tis true.

GUIDERIUS.

Come on, then, and remove him.

ARVIRAGUS.

So. Begin.

SONG

GUIDERIUS.

Fear no more the heat o' th' sun,
 Nor the furious winter's rages;
Thou thy worldly task hast done,
 Home art gone, and ta'en thy wages.
Golden lads and girls all must,
As chimney-sweepers, come to dust.

ARVIRAGUS.

Fear no more the frown o' th' great;
 Thou art past the tyrant's stroke.
Care no more to clothe and eat;
 To thee the reed is as the oak.
The sceptre, learning, physic, must
All follow this and come to dust.

GUIDERIUS.

Fear no more the lightning flash.

ARVIRAGUS.

Nor th' all-dreaded thunder-stone.

GUIDERIUS.

Fear not slander, censure rash;

ARVIRAGUS.

Thou hast finish'd joy and moan.

BOTH.

All lovers young, all lovers must

Consign to thee and come to dust.

GUIDERIUS.

No exorciser harm thee!

ARVIRAGUS.

Nor no witchcraft charm thee!

GUIDERIUS.

Ghost unlaid forbear thee!

ARVIRAGUS.

Nothing ill come near thee!

BOTH.

Quiet consummation have,

And renowned be thy grave!

Enter Belarius with the body of Cloten.

GUIDERIUS.

We have done our obsequies. Come, lay him down.

BELARIUS.

Here's a few flowers; but 'bout midnight, more.

The herbs that have on them cold dew o' th' night

Are strewings fit'st for graves. Upon their faces.

You were as flow'rs, now wither'd. Even so

These herblets shall which we upon you strew.

Come on, away. Apart upon our knees.

The ground that gave them first has them again.

Their pleasures here are past, so is their pain.

> [Exeunt all but Imogen.]

IMOGEN.

[Awaking.] Yes, sir, to Milford Haven. Which is the way?

I thank you. By yond bush? Pray, how far thither?

'Ods pittikins! can it be six mile yet?

I have gone all night. Faith, I'll lie down and sleep.

But, soft! no bedfellow. O gods and goddesses!

> [Seeing the body.]

These flow'rs are like the pleasures of the world;

This bloody man, the care on't. I hope I dream;

For so I thought I was a cave-keeper,

And cook to honest creatures. But 'tis not so;

'Twas but a bolt of nothing, shot at nothing,

Which the brain makes of fumes. Our very eyes

Are sometimes, like our judgements, blind. Good faith,

I tremble still with fear; but if there be

Yet left in heaven as small a drop of pity

As a wren's eye, fear'd gods, a part of it!

The dream's here still. Even when I wake it is

Without me, as within me; not imagin'd, felt.

A headless man? The garments of Posthumus?

I know the shape of's leg; this is his hand,

His foot Mercurial, his Martial thigh,

The brawns of Hercules; but his Jovial face—

Murder in heaven! How! 'Tis gone. Pisanio,

All curses madded Hecuba gave the Greeks,

And mine to boot, be darted on thee! Thou,

Conspir'd with that irregulous devil, Cloten,

Hath here cut off my lord. To write and read

Be henceforth treacherous! Damn'd Pisanio

Hath with his forged letters (damn'd Pisanio)

From this most bravest vessel of the world

Struck the main-top. O Posthumus! alas,

Where is thy head? Where's that? Ay me! where's that?

Pisanio might have kill'd thee at the heart,

And left this head on. How should this be? Pisanio?

'Tis he and Cloten; malice and lucre in them

Have laid this woe here. O, 'tis pregnant, pregnant!

The drug he gave me, which he said was precious

And cordial to me, have I not found it

Murd'rous to th' senses? That confirms it home.

This is Pisanio's deed, and Cloten. O!

Give colour to my pale cheek with thy blood,

That we the horrider may seem to those

Which chance to find us. O, my lord, my lord!

[Falls fainting on the body.]

Enter Lucius, Captains and a Soothsayer.

CAPTAIN.

To them the legions garrison'd in Gallia,

After your will, have cross'd the sea, attending

You here at Milford Haven; with your ships,

They are in readiness.

LUCIUS.

But what from Rome?

CAPTAIN.

The Senate hath stirr'd up the confiners

And gentlemen of Italy, most willing spirits,

That promise noble service; and they come

Under the conduct of bold Iachimo,

Sienna's brother.

LUCIUS.

When expect you them?

CAPTAIN.

With the next benefit o' th' wind.

LUCIUS.

This forwardness

Makes our hopes fair. Command our present numbers

Be muster'd; bid the captains look to't. Now, sir,

What have you dream'd of late of this war's purpose?

SOOTHSAYER.

Last night the very gods show'd me a vision

(I fast and pray'd for their intelligence) thus:

I saw Jove's bird, the Roman eagle, wing'd

From the spongy south to this part of the west,

There vanish'd in the sunbeams; which portends,

Unless my sins abuse my divination,

Success to th' Roman host.

LUCIUS.

Dream often so,

And never false. Soft, ho! what trunk is here

Without his top? The ruin speaks that sometime

It was a worthy building. How? a page?

Or dead or sleeping on him? But dead, rather;

For nature doth abhor to make his bed

With the defunct, or sleep upon the dead.

Let's see the boy's face.

CAPTAIN.

He's alive, my lord.

LUCIUS.

He'll then instruct us of this body. Young one,

Inform us of thy fortunes; for it seems

They crave to be demanded. Who is this

Thou mak'st thy bloody pillow? Or who was he

That, otherwise than noble nature did,

Hath alter'd that good picture? What's thy interest

In this sad wreck? How came't? Who is't?

What art thou?

IMOGEN.

I am nothing; or if not,

Nothing to be were better. This was my master,

A very valiant Briton and a good,

That here by mountaineers lies slain. Alas!

There is no more such masters. I may wander

From east to occident; cry out for service;

Try many, all good; serve truly; never

Find such another master.

LUCIUS.

'Lack, good youth!

Thou mov'st no less with thy complaining than

Thy master in bleeding. Say his name, good friend.

IMOGEN.

Richard du Champ. [Aside.] If I do lie, and do

No harm by it, though the gods hear, I hope

They'll pardon it.—Say you, sir?

LUCIUS.

Thy name?

IMOGEN.

Fidele, sir.

LUCIUS.

Thou dost approve thyself the very same;

Thy name well fits thy faith, thy faith thy name.

Wilt take thy chance with me? I will not say

Thou shalt be so well master'd; but, be sure,

No less belov'd. The Roman Emperor's letters,

Sent by a consul to me, should not sooner

Than thine own worth prefer thee. Go with me.

IMOGEN.

I'll follow, sir. But first, an't please the gods,

I'll hide my master from the flies, as deep

As these poor pickaxes can dig; and when

With wild wood-leaves and weeds I ha' strew'd his grave,

And on it said a century of prayers,

Such as I can, twice o'er, I'll weep and sigh;

And leaving so his service, follow you,

So please you entertain me.

LUCIUS.

Ay, good youth;

And rather father thee than master thee.

My friends,

The boy hath taught us manly duties; let us

Find out the prettiest daisied plot we can,

And make him with our pikes and partisans

A grave. Come, arm him. Boy, he is preferr'd

By thee to us; and he shall be interr'd

As soldiers can. Be cheerful; wipe thine eyes.

Some falls are means the happier to arise.

[Exeunt.]

SCENE III. Britain. Cymbeline's palace.

Enter Cymbeline, Lords, Pisanio and Attendants.

CYMBELINE.

Again! and bring me word how 'tis with her.

[Exit an Attendant.]

A fever with the absence of her son;

A madness, of which her life's in danger. Heavens,

How deeply you at once do touch me! Imogen,

The great part of my comfort, gone; my queen

Upon a desperate bed, and in a time

When fearful wars point at me; her son gone,

So needful for this present. It strikes me past

The hope of comfort. But for thee, fellow,

Who needs must know of her departure and

Dost seem so ignorant, we'll enforce it from thee

By a sharp torture.

PISANIO.

Sir, my life is yours;

I humbly set it at your will; but for my mistress,

I nothing know where she remains, why gone,

Nor when she purposes return. Beseech your Highness,

Hold me your loyal servant.

LORD.

Good my liege,

The day that she was missing he was here.

I dare be bound he's true and shall perform

All parts of his subjection loyally. For Cloten,

There wants no diligence in seeking him,

And will no doubt be found.

CYMBELINE.

The time is troublesome.

[To Pisanio.] We'll slip you for a season; but our jealousy

Does yet depend.

LORD.

So please your Majesty,

The Roman legions, all from Gallia drawn,

Are landed on your coast, with a supply

Of Roman gentlemen by the Senate sent.

CYMBELINE.

Now for the counsel of my son and queen!

I am amaz'd with matter.

LORD.

Good my liege,

Your preparation can affront no less

Than what you hear of. Come more, for more you're ready.

The want is but to put those pow'rs in motion

That long to move.

CYMBELINE.

I thank you. Let's withdraw,

And meet the time as it seeks us. We fear not

What can from Italy annoy us; but

We grieve at chances here. Away!

[Exeunt all but Pisanio.]

PISANIO.

I heard no letter from my master since

I wrote him Imogen was slain. 'Tis strange.

Nor hear I from my mistress, who did promise

To yield me often tidings. Neither know I

What is betid to Cloten, but remain

Perplex'd in all. The heavens still must work.

Wherein I am false I am honest; not true, to be true.

These present wars shall find I love my country,

Even to the note o' th' King, or I'll fall in them.

All other doubts, by time let them be clear'd:

Fortune brings in some boats that are not steer'd.

[Exit.]

SCENE IV. Wales. Before the cave of Belarius.

Enter Belarius, Guiderius and Arviragus.

GUIDERIUS.

The noise is round about us.

BELARIUS.

Let us from it.

ARVIRAGUS.

What pleasure, sir, find we in life, to lock it

From action and adventure?

GUIDERIUS.

Nay, what hope

Have we in hiding us? This way the Romans

Must or for Britons slay us, or receive us

For barbarous and unnatural revolts

During their use, and slay us after.

BELARIUS.

Sons,

We'll higher to the mountains; there secure us.

To the King's party there's no going. Newness

Of Cloten's death (we being not known, not muster'd

Among the bands) may drive us to a render

Where we have liv'd, and so extort from's that

Which we have done, whose answer would be death,

Drawn on with torture.

GUIDERIUS.

This is, sir, a doubt

In such a time nothing becoming you

Nor satisfying us.

ARVIRAGUS.

It is not likely

That when they hear the Roman horses neigh,

Behold their quarter'd fires, have both their eyes

And ears so cloy'd importantly as now,

That they will waste their time upon our note,

To know from whence we are.

BELARIUS.

O, I am known

Of many in the army. Many years,

Though Cloten then but young, you see, not wore him

From my remembrance. And, besides, the King

Hath not deserv'd my service nor your loves,

Who find in my exile the want of breeding,

The certainty of this hard life; aye hopeless

To have the courtesy your cradle promis'd,

But to be still hot summer's tanlings and

The shrinking slaves of winter.

GUIDERIUS.

Than be so,

Better to cease to be. Pray, sir, to th' army.

I and my brother are not known; yourself

So out of thought, and thereto so o'ergrown,

Cannot be questioned.

ARVIRAGUS.

By this sun that shines,

I'll thither. What thing is't that I never

Did see man die! scarce ever look'd on blood

But that of coward hares, hot goats, and venison!

Never bestrid a horse, save one that had

A rider like myself, who ne'er wore rowel

Nor iron on his heel! I am asham'd

To look upon the holy sun, to have

The benefit of his blest beams, remaining

So long a poor unknown.

GUIDERIUS.

By heavens, I'll go!

If you will bless me, sir, and give me leave,

I'll take the better care; but if you will not,

The hazard therefore due fall on me by

The hands of Romans!

ARVIRAGUS.

So say I. Amen.

BELARIUS.

No reason I, since of your lives you set

So slight a valuation, should reserve

My crack'd one to more care. Have with you, boys!

If in your country wars you chance to die,

That is my bed too, lads, and there I'll lie.

Lead, lead. [Aside.] The time seems long; their blood thinks scorn

Till it fly out and show them princes born.

[Exeunt.]

ACT V

SCENE I. Britain. The Roman camp.

Enter Posthumus alone, with a bloody handkerchief.

POSTHUMUS.

Yea, bloody cloth, I'll keep thee; for I wish'd

Thou shouldst be colour'd thus. You married ones,

If each of you should take this course, how many

Must murder wives much better than themselves

For wrying but a little! O Pisanio!

Every good servant does not all commands;

No bond but to do just ones. Gods! if you

Should have ta'en vengeance on my faults, I never

Had liv'd to put on this; so had you saved

The noble Imogen to repent, and struck

Me, wretch more worth your vengeance. But alack,

You snatch some hence for little faults; that's love,

To have them fall no more. You some permit

To second ills with ills, each elder worse,

And make them dread it, to the doers' thrift.

But Imogen is your own. Do your best wills,

And make me blest to obey. I am brought hither

Among th' Italian gentry, and to fight

Against my lady's kingdom. 'Tis enough

That, Britain, I have kill'd thy mistress; peace!

I'll give no wound to thee. Therefore, good heavens,

Hear patiently my purpose. I'll disrobe me

Of these Italian weeds, and suit myself

As does a Britain peasant. So I'll fight

Against the part I come with; so I'll die

For thee, O Imogen, even for whom my life

Is every breath a death. And thus unknown,

Pitied nor hated, to the face of peril

Myself I'll dedicate. Let me make men know

More valour in me than my habits show.

Gods, put the strength o' th' Leonati in me!

To shame the guise o' th' world, I will begin

The fashion less without and more within.

[Exit.]

SCENE II. Britain. A field of battle between the British and Roman camps.

Enter Lucius, Iachimo and the Roman army at one door, and the British army at another, Leonatus Posthumus following like a poor soldier. They march over and go out. Alarums. Then enter again, in skirmish, Iachimo and Posthumus. He vanquisheth and disarmeth Iachimo and then leaves him.

IACHIMO.

The heaviness and guilt within my bosom

Takes off my manhood. I have belied a lady,

The Princess of this country, and the air on't

Revengingly enfeebles me; or could this carl,

A very drudge of nature's, have subdu'd me

In my profession? Knighthoods and honours borne

As I wear mine are titles but of scorn.

If that thy gentry, Britain, go before

This lout as he exceeds our lords, the odds

Is that we scarce are men, and you are gods.

[Exit.]

The battle continues; the Britons fly; Cymbeline is taken. Then enter to his rescue Belarius, Guiderius and Arviragus.

BELARIUS.

Stand, stand! We have th' advantage of the ground;

The lane is guarded; nothing routs us but

The villainy of our fears.

GUIDERIUS and ARVIRAGUS.

Stand, stand, and fight!

Enter Posthumus and seconds the Britons; they rescue Cymbeline and exeunt. Then re-enter Lucius and Iachimo with Imogen.

LUCIUS.

Away, boy, from the troops, and save thyself;

For friends kill friends, and the disorder's such

As war were hoodwink'd.

IACHIMO.

'Tis their fresh supplies.

LUCIUS.

It is a day turn'd strangely. Or betimes

Let's reinforce or fly.

[Exeunt.]

SCENE III. Another part of the field.

Enter Posthumus and a Briton Lord.

LORD.

Cam'st thou from where they made the stand?

POSTHUMUS.

I did:

Though you, it seems, come from the fliers.

LORD.

I did.

POSTHUMUS.

No blame be to you, sir, for all was lost,

But that the heavens fought. The King himself

Of his wings destitute, the army broken,

And but the backs of Britons seen, all flying,

Through a strait lane; the enemy, full-hearted,

Lolling the tongue with slaught'ring, having work

More plentiful than tools to do't, struck down

Some mortally, some slightly touch'd, some falling

Merely through fear, that the strait pass was damm'd

With dead men hurt behind, and cowards living

To die with length'ned shame.

LORD.

Where was this lane?

POSTHUMUS.

Close by the battle, ditch'd, and wall'd with turf,

Which gave advantage to an ancient soldier,

An honest one, I warrant, who deserv'd

So long a breeding as his white beard came to,

In doing this for's country. Athwart the lane

He, with two striplings (lads more like to run

The country base than to commit such slaughter;

With faces fit for masks, or rather fairer

Than those for preservation cas'd or shame)

Made good the passage, cried to those that fled

'Our Britain's harts die flying, not our men.

To darkness fleet souls that fly backwards! Stand;

Or we are Romans and will give you that,

Like beasts, which you shun beastly, and may save

But to look back in frown. Stand, stand!' These three,

Three thousand confident, in act as many—

For three performers are the file when all

The rest do nothing—with this word 'Stand, stand!'

Accommodated by the place, more charming

With their own nobleness, which could have turn'd

A distaff to a lance, gilded pale looks,

Part shame, part spirit renew'd; that some turn'd coward

But by example (O, a sin in war

Damn'd in the first beginners) 'gan to look

The way that they did and to grin like lions

Upon the pikes o' th' hunters. Then began

A stop i' th' chaser, a retire; anon

A rout, confusion thick. Forthwith they fly,

Chickens, the way which they stoop'd eagles; slaves,

The strides they victors made; and now our cowards,

Like fragments in hard voyages, became

The life o' th' need. Having found the back-door open

Of the unguarded hearts, heavens, how they wound!

Some slain before, some dying, some their friends

O'erborne i' th' former wave. Ten chas'd by one

Are now each one the slaughterman of twenty.

Those that would die or ere resist are grown

The mortal bugs o' th' field.

LORD.

This was strange chance:

A narrow lane, an old man, and two boys.

POSTHUMUS.

Nay, do not wonder at it; you are made

Rather to wonder at the things you hear

Than to work any. Will you rhyme upon't,

And vent it for a mock'ry? Here is one:

> 'Two boys, an old man (twice a boy), a lane,

> Preserv'd the Britons, was the Romans' bane.'

LORD.

Nay, be not angry, sir.

POSTHUMUS.

'Lack, to what end?

Who dares not stand his foe I'll be his friend;

For if he'll do as he is made to do,

I know he'll quickly fly my friendship too.

You have put me into rhyme.

LORD.

Farewell; you're angry.

[Exit.]

POSTHUMUS.

Still going? This is a lord! O noble misery,

To be i' th' field and ask 'What news?' of me!

Today how many would have given their honours

To have sav'd their carcasses! took heel to do't,

And yet died too! I, in mine own woe charm'd,

Could not find death where I did hear him groan,

Nor feel him where he struck. Being an ugly monster,

'Tis strange he hides him in fresh cups, soft beds,

Sweet words; or hath moe ministers than we

That draw his knives i' th' war. Well, I will find him;

For being now a favourer to the Briton,

No more a Briton, I have resum'd again

The part I came in. Fight I will no more,

But yield me to the veriest hind that shall

Once touch my shoulder. Great the slaughter is

Here made by th' Roman; great the answer be

Britons must take. For me, my ransom's death;

On either side I come to spend my breath,

Which neither here I'll keep nor bear again,

But end it by some means for Imogen.

Enter two British Captains and soldiers.

FIRST CAPTAIN.

Great Jupiter be prais'd! Lucius is taken.

'Tis thought the old man and his sons were angels.

SECOND CAPTAIN.

There was a fourth man, in a silly habit,

That gave th' affront with them.

FIRST CAPTAIN.

So 'tis reported;

But none of 'em can be found. Stand! who's there?

POSTHUMUS.

A Roman,

Who had not now been drooping here if seconds

Had answer'd him.

SECOND CAPTAIN.

Lay hands on him; a dog!

A leg of Rome shall not return to tell

What crows have peck'd them here. He brags his service,

As if he were of note. Bring him to th' King.

Enter Cymbeline, Belarius, Guiderius, Arviragus, Pisanio and Roman captives. The Captains present Posthumus to Cymbeline, who delivers him over to a gaoler.

[Exeunt omnes.]

SCENE IV. Britain. A prison.

Enter Posthumus and two Gaolers.

FIRST GAOLER. You shall not now be stol'n, you have locks upon you;

So graze as you find pasture.

SECOND GAOLER.

Ay, or a stomach.

[Exeunt Gaolers.]

POSTHUMUS.

Most welcome, bondage! for thou art a way,

I think, to liberty. Yet am I better

Than one that's sick o' th' gout, since he had rather

Groan so in perpetuity than be cur'd

By th' sure physician death, who is the key

T' unbar these locks. My conscience, thou art fetter'd

More than my shanks and wrists; you good gods, give me

The penitent instrument to pick that bolt,

Then, free for ever! Is't enough I am sorry?

So children temporal fathers do appease;

Gods are more full of mercy. Must I repent,

I cannot do it better than in gyves,

Desir'd more than constrain'd. To satisfy,

If of my freedom 'tis the main part, take

No stricter render of me than my all.

I know you are more clement than vile men,

Who of their broken debtors take a third,

A sixth, a tenth, letting them thrive again

On their abatement; that's not my desire.

For Imogen's dear life take mine; and though

'Tis not so dear, yet 'tis a life; you coin'd it.

'Tween man and man they weigh not every stamp;

Though light, take pieces for the figure's sake;

You rather mine, being yours. And so, great pow'rs,

If you will take this audit, take this life,

And cancel these cold bonds. O Imogen!

I'll speak to thee in silence.

[Sleeps.]

Solemn music. Enter, as in an apparition, Sicilius Leonatus, father to Posthumus, an old man attired like a warrior; leading in his hand an ancient matron, his wife and Mother to Posthumus, with music before them. Then, after other music, follows the two young Leonati, brothers to Posthumus, with wounds, as they died in the wars. They circle Posthumus round as he lies sleeping.

SICILIUS.

No more, thou thunder-master, show

Thy spite on mortal flies.

With Mars fall out, with Juno chide,

That thy adulteries

Rates and revenges.

Hath my poor boy done aught but well,

Whose face I never saw?

I died whilst in the womb he stay'd

Attending nature's law;

Whose father then, as men report

Thou orphans' father art,

Thou shouldst have been, and shielded him

From this earth-vexing smart.

MOTHER.

Lucina lent not me her aid,

But took me in my throes,

That from me was Posthumus ripp'd,

Came crying 'mongst his foes,

A thing of pity.

SICILIUS.

Great Nature like his ancestry

Moulded the stuff so fair

That he deserv'd the praise o' th' world

As great Sicilius' heir.

FIRST BROTHER.

When once he was mature for man,

In Britain where was he

That could stand up his parallel,

Or fruitful object be

In eye of Imogen, that best

Could deem his dignity?

MOTHER.

With marriage wherefore was he mock'd,

To be exil'd and thrown

From Leonati seat and cast

From her his dearest one,

Sweet Imogen?

SICILIUS.

Why did you suffer Iachimo,

Slight thing of Italy,

To taint his nobler heart and brain

With needless jealousy,

And to become the geck and scorn

O' th' other's villainy?

SECOND BROTHER.

For this from stiller seats we came,

Our parents and us twain,

That, striking in our country's cause,

Fell bravely and were slain,

Our fealty and Tenantius' right

With honour to maintain.

FIRST BROTHER.

Like hardiment Posthumus hath

To Cymbeline perform'd.

Then, Jupiter, thou king of gods,

Why hast thou thus adjourn'd

The graces for his merits due,

Being all to dolours turn'd?

SICILIUS.

Thy crystal window ope; look out;

No longer exercise

Upon a valiant race thy harsh

And potent injuries.

MOTHER.

Since, Jupiter, our son is good,

Take off his miseries.

SICILIUS.

Peep through thy marble mansion. Help!

Or we poor ghosts will cry

To th' shining synod of the rest

Against thy deity.

BROTHERS.

Help, Jupiter! or we appeal,

And from thy justice fly.

Jupiter descends in thunder and lightning, sitting upon an eagle. He throws a thunderbolt. The Ghosts fall on their knees.

JUPITER.

No more, you petty spirits of region low,

Offend our hearing; hush! How dare you ghosts

Accuse the Thunderer whose bolt, you know,

Sky-planted, batters all rebelling coasts?

Poor shadows of Elysium, hence and rest

Upon your never-withering banks of flow'rs.

Be not with mortal accidents opprest:

No care of yours it is; you know 'tis ours.

Whom best I love I cross; to make my gift,

The more delay'd, delighted. Be content;

Your low-laid son our godhead will uplift;

His comforts thrive, his trials well are spent.

Our Jovial star reign'd at his birth, and in

Our temple was he married. Rise and fade!

He shall be lord of Lady Imogen,

And happier much by his affliction made.

This tablet lay upon his breast, wherein

Our pleasure his full fortune doth confine;

And so, away; no farther with your din

Express impatience, lest you stir up mine.

Mount, eagle, to my palace crystalline.

[Ascends.]

SICILIUS.

He came in thunder; his celestial breath

Was sulphurous to smell; the holy eagle

Stoop'd as to foot us. His ascension is

More sweet than our blest fields. His royal bird

Prunes the immortal wing, and cloys his beak,

As when his god is pleas'd.

ALL.

Thanks, Jupiter!

SICILIUS.

The marble pavement closes, he is enter'd

His radiant roof. Away! and, to be blest,

Let us with care perform his great behest.

[Ghosts vanish.]

POSTHUMUS.

[Waking.] Sleep, thou has been a grandsire and begot

A father to me; and thou hast created

A mother and two brothers. But, O scorn,

Gone! They went hence so soon as they were born.

And so I am awake. Poor wretches, that depend

On greatness' favour, dream as I have done;

Wake and find nothing. But, alas, I swerve;

Many dream not to find, neither deserve,

And yet are steep'd in favours; so am I,

That have this golden chance, and know not why.

What fairies haunt this ground? A book? O rare one!

Be not, as is our fangled world, a garment

Nobler than that it covers. Let thy effects

So follow to be most unlike our courtiers,

As good as promise.

[Reads.] When as a lion's whelp shall, to himself unknown, without seeking find, and be embrac'd by a piece of tender air; and when from a stately cedar shall be lopp'd branches which, being dead many years, shall after revive, be jointed to the old stock, and freshly grow; then shall Posthumus end his miseries, Britain be fortunate and flourish in peace and plenty.

'Tis still a dream, or else such stuff as madmen

Tongue, and brain not; either both or nothing,

Or senseless speaking, or a speaking such

As sense cannot untie. Be what it is,

The action of my life is like it, which

I'll keep, if but for sympathy.

Enter Gaoler.

GAOLER.

Come, sir, are you ready for death?

POSTHUMUS.

Over-roasted rather; ready long ago.

GAOLER.

Hanging is the word, sir; if you be ready for that, you are well cook'd.

POSTHUMUS.

So, if I prove a good repast to the spectators, the dish pays the shot.

GAOLER.

A heavy reckoning for you, sir. But the comfort is, you shall be called to no more payments, fear no more tavern bills, which are often the sadness of parting, as the procuring of mirth. You come in faint for want of meat, depart reeling with too much drink; sorry that you have paid too much, and sorry that you are paid too much; purse and brain both empty; the brain the heavier for being too light, the purse too light, being drawn of heaviness. O, of this contradiction you shall now be quit. O, the charity of a penny cord! It sums up thousands in a trice. You have no true debitor and creditor but it; of what's past, is, and to come, the discharge. Your neck, sir, is pen, book, and counters; so the acquittance follows.

POSTHUMUS.

I am merrier to die than thou art to live.

GAOLER.

Indeed, sir, he that sleeps feels not the toothache. But a man that were to sleep your sleep, and a hangman to help him to bed, I think he would change places with his officer; for look you, sir, you know not which way you shall go.

POSTHUMUS.

Yes indeed do I, fellow.

GAOLER.

Your death has eyes in's head, then; I have not seen him so pictur'd. You must either be directed by some that take upon them to know, or to take upon yourself that which I am sure you do not know, or jump the after-inquiry on your own peril. And how you shall speed in your journey's end, I think you'll never return to tell one.

POSTHUMUS.

I tell thee, fellow, there are none want eyes to direct them the way I am going, but such as wink and will not use them.

GAOLER.

What an infinite mock is this, that a man should have the best use of eyes to see the way of blindness! I am sure hanging's the way of winking.

Enter a Messenger.

MESSENGER.

Knock off his manacles; bring your prisoner to the King.

POSTHUMUS.

Thou bring'st good news: I am call'd to be made free.

GAOLER.

I'll be hang'd then.

POSTHUMUS.

Thou shalt be then freer than a gaoler; no bolts for the dead.

[Exeunt Posthumus and Messenger.]

GAOLER.

Unless a man would marry a gallows and beget young gibbets, I never saw one so prone. Yet, on my conscience, there are verier knaves desire to live, for all he be a Roman; and there be some of them too that die against their wills; so should I, if I were one. I would we were all of one mind, and one mind good. O, there were desolation of gaolers and gallowses! I speak against my present profit, but my wish hath a preferment in't.

[Exit.]

SCENE V. Britain. Cymbeline's tent.

Enter Cymbeline, Belarius, Guiderius, Arviragus, Pisanio, Lords, Officers and Attendants.

CYMBELINE.

Stand by my side, you whom the gods have made

Preservers of my throne. Woe is my heart

That the poor soldier that so richly fought,

Whose rags sham'd gilded arms, whose naked breast

Stepp'd before targes of proof, cannot be found.

He shall be happy that can find him, if

Our grace can make him so.

BELARIUS.

I never saw

Such noble fury in so poor a thing;

Such precious deeds in one that promis'd nought

But beggary and poor looks.

CYMBELINE.

No tidings of him?

PISANIO.

He hath been search'd among the dead and living,

But no trace of him.

CYMBELINE.

To my grief, I am

The heir of his reward, [To Belarius, Guiderius, and Arviragus] which I will add

To you, the liver, heart, and brain of Britain,

By whom I grant she lives. 'Tis now the time

To ask of whence you are. Report it.

BELARIUS.

Sir,

In Cambria are we born, and gentlemen;

Further to boast were neither true nor modest,

Unless I add we are honest.

CYMBELINE.

Bow your knees.

Arise my knights o' th' battle; I create you

Companions to our person, and will fit you

With dignities becoming your estates.

Enter Cornelius and Ladies.

There's business in these faces. Why so sadly

Greet you our victory? You look like Romans,

And not o' th' court of Britain.

CORNELIUS.

Hail, great King!

To sour your happiness I must report

The Queen is dead.

CYMBELINE.

Who worse than a physician

Would this report become? But I consider

By med'cine life may be prolong'd, yet death

Will seize the doctor too. How ended she?

CORNELIUS.

With horror, madly dying, like her life;

Which, being cruel to the world, concluded

Most cruel to herself. What she confess'd

I will report, so please you; these her women

Can trip me if I err, who with wet cheeks

Were present when she finish'd.

CYMBELINE.

Prithee say.

CORNELIUS.

First, she confess'd she never lov'd you; only

Affected greatness got by you, not you;

Married your royalty, was wife to your place;

Abhorr'd your person.

CYMBELINE.

She alone knew this;

And but she spoke it dying, I would not

Believe her lips in opening it. Proceed.

CORNELIUS.

Your daughter, whom she bore in hand to love

With such integrity, she did confess

Was as a scorpion to her sight; whose life,

But that her flight prevented it, she had

Ta'en off by poison.

CYMBELINE.

O most delicate fiend!

Who is't can read a woman? Is there more?

CORNELIUS.

More, sir, and worse. She did confess she had

For you a mortal mineral, which, being took,

Should by the minute feed on life, and ling'ring,

By inches waste you. In which time she purpos'd,

By watching, weeping, tendance, kissing, to

O'ercome you with her show; and in time,

When she had fitted you with her craft, to work

Her son into th' adoption of the crown;

But failing of her end by his strange absence,

Grew shameless-desperate, open'd, in despite

Of heaven and men, her purposes, repented

The evils she hatch'd were not effected; so,

Despairing, died.

CYMBELINE.

Heard you all this, her women?

LADIES.

We did, so please your Highness.

CYMBELINE.

Mine eyes

Were not in fault, for she was beautiful;

Mine ears, that heard her flattery; nor my heart

That thought her like her seeming. It had been vicious

To have mistrusted her; yet, O my daughter!

That it was folly in me thou mayst say,

And prove it in thy feeling. Heaven mend all!

Enter Lucius, Iachimo, the Soothsayer and other Roman prisoners, guarded; Posthumus behind, and Imogen.

Thou com'st not, Caius, now for tribute; that

The Britons have raz'd out, though with the loss

Of many a bold one, whose kinsmen have made suit

That their good souls may be appeas'd with slaughter

Of you their captives, which ourself have granted;

So think of your estate.

LUCIUS.

Consider, sir, the chance of war. The day

Was yours by accident; had it gone with us,

We should not, when the blood was cool, have threaten'd

Our prisoners with the sword. But since the gods

Will have it thus, that nothing but our lives

May be call'd ransom, let it come. Sufficeth

A Roman with a Roman's heart can suffer.

Augustus lives to think on't; and so much

For my peculiar care. This one thing only

I will entreat: my boy, a Briton born,

Let him be ransom'd. Never master had

A page so kind, so duteous, diligent,

So tender over his occasions, true,

So feat, so nurse-like; let his virtue join

With my request, which I'll make bold your Highness

Cannot deny; he hath done no Briton harm

Though he have serv'd a Roman. Save him, sir,

And spare no blood beside.

CYMBELINE.

I have surely seen him;

His favour is familiar to me. Boy,

Thou hast look'd thyself into my grace,

And art mine own. I know not why, wherefore

To say "Live, boy." Ne'er thank thy master. Live;

And ask of Cymbeline what boon thou wilt,

Fitting my bounty and thy state, I'll give it;

Yea, though thou do demand a prisoner,

The noblest ta'en.

IMOGEN.

I humbly thank your Highness.

LUCIUS.

I do not bid thee beg my life, good lad,

And yet I know thou wilt.

IMOGEN.

No, no! Alack,

There's other work in hand. I see a thing

Bitter to me as death; your life, good master,

Must shuffle for itself.

LUCIUS.

The boy disdains me,

He leaves me, scorns me. Briefly die their joys

That place them on the truth of girls and boys.

Why stands he so perplex'd?

CYMBELINE.

What wouldst thou, boy?

I love thee more and more; think more and more

What's best to ask. Know'st him thou look'st on? Speak,

Wilt have him live? Is he thy kin? thy friend?

IMOGEN.

He is a Roman, no more kin to me

Than I to your Highness; who, being born your vassal,

Am something nearer.

CYMBELINE.

Wherefore ey'st him so?

IMOGEN.

I'll tell you, sir, in private, if you please

To give me hearing.

CYMBELINE.

Ay, with all my heart,

And lend my best attention. What's thy name?

IMOGEN.

Fidele, sir.

CYMBELINE.

Thou'rt my good youth, my page;

I'll be thy master. Walk with me; speak freely.

       [Cymbeline and Imogen converse apart.]

BELARIUS.

Is not this boy reviv'd from death?

ARVIRAGUS.

One sand another

Not more resembles that sweet rosy lad

Who died and was Fidele. What think you?

GUIDERIUS.

The same dead thing alive.

BELARIUS.

Peace, peace! see further. He eyes us not; forbear.

Creatures may be alike; were't he, I am sure

He would have spoke to us.

GUIDERIUS.

But we see him dead.

BELARIUS.

Be silent; let's see further.

PISANIO.

[Aside.] It is my mistress.

Since she is living, let the time run on

To good or bad.

[Cymbeline and Imogen advance.]

CYMBELINE.

Come, stand thou by our side;

Make thy demand aloud. [To Iachimo.] Sir, step you forth;

Give answer to this boy, and do it freely,

Or, by our greatness and the grace of it,

Which is our honour, bitter torture shall

Winnow the truth from falsehood. On, speak to him.

IMOGEN.

My boon is that this gentleman may render

Of whom he had this ring.

POSTHUMUS.

[Aside.] What's that to him?

CYMBELINE.

That diamond upon your finger, say

How came it yours?

IACHIMO.

Thou'lt torture me to leave unspoken that

Which to be spoke would torture thee.

CYMBELINE.

How? me?

IACHIMO.

I am glad to be constrain'd to utter that

Which torments me to conceal. By villainy

I got this ring; 'twas Leonatus' jewel,

Whom thou didst banish; and—which more may grieve thee,

As it doth me—a nobler sir ne'er liv'd

'Twixt sky and ground. Wilt thou hear more, my lord?

CYMBELINE.

All that belongs to this.

IACHIMO.

That paragon, thy daughter,

For whom my heart drops blood and my false spirits

Quail to remember—Give me leave, I faint.

CYMBELINE.

My daughter? What of her? Renew thy strength;

I had rather thou shouldst live while nature will

Than die ere I hear more. Strive, man, and speak.

IACHIMO.

Upon a time, unhappy was the clock

That struck the hour: was in Rome, accurs'd

The mansion where: 'twas at a feast, O, would

Our viands had been poison'd (or at least

Those which I heav'd to head) the good Posthumus

(What should I say? he was too good to be

Where ill men were, and was the best of all

Amongst the rar'st of good ones) sitting sadly

Hearing us praise our loves of Italy

For beauty that made barren the swell'd boast

Of him that best could speak; for feature, laming

The shrine of Venus or straight-pight Minerva,

Postures beyond brief nature; for condition,

A shop of all the qualities that man

Loves woman for; besides that hook of wiving,

Fairness which strikes the eye.

CYMBELINE.

I stand on fire.

Come to the matter.

IACHIMO.

All too soon I shall,

Unless thou wouldst grieve quickly. This Posthumus,

Most like a noble lord in love and one

That had a royal lover, took his hint;

And (not dispraising whom we prais'd, therein

He was as calm as virtue) he began

His mistress' picture; which by his tongue being made,

And then a mind put in't, either our brags

Were crack'd of kitchen trulls, or his description

Prov'd us unspeaking sots.

CYMBELINE.

Nay, nay, to th' purpose.

IACHIMO.

Your daughter's chastity (there it begins)

He spake of her as Dian had hot dreams

And she alone were cold; whereat I, wretch,

Made scruple of his praise, and wager'd with him

Pieces of gold 'gainst this which then he wore

Upon his honour'd finger, to attain

In suit the place of's bed, and win this ring

By hers and mine adultery. He, true knight,

No lesser of her honour confident

Than I did truly find her, stakes this ring;

And would so, had it been a carbuncle

Of Phoebus' wheel; and might so safely, had it

Been all the worth of's car. Away to Britain

Post I in this design. Well may you, sir,

Remember me at court, where I was taught

Of your chaste daughter the wide difference

'Twixt amorous and villainous. Being thus quench'd

Of hope, not longing, mine Italian brain

Gan in your duller Britain operate

Most vilely; for my vantage, excellent;

And, to be brief, my practice so prevail'd

That I return'd with simular proof enough

To make the noble Leonatus mad,

By wounding his belief in her renown

With tokens thus and thus; averring notes

Of chamber-hanging, pictures, this her bracelet

(O cunning, how I got it!) nay, some marks

Of secret on her person, that he could not

But think her bond of chastity quite crack'd,

I having ta'en the forfeit. Whereupon

Methinks I see him now—

POSTHUMUS.

[Coming forward.] Ay, so thou dost,

Italian fiend! Ay me, most credulous fool,

Egregious murderer, thief, anything

That's due to all the villains past, in being,

To come! O, give me cord, or knife, or poison,

Some upright justicer! Thou, King, send out

For torturers ingenious. It is I

That all th' abhorred things o' th' earth amend

By being worse than they. I am Posthumus,

That kill'd thy daughter; villain-like, I lie;

That caus'd a lesser villain than myself,

A sacrilegious thief, to do't. The temple

Of virtue was she; yea, and she herself.

Spit, and throw stones, cast mire upon me, set

The dogs o' th' street to bay me. Every villain

Be call'd Posthumus Leonatus, and

Be villainy less than 'twas! O Imogen!

My queen, my life, my wife! O Imogen,

Imogen, Imogen!

IMOGEN.

Peace, my lord. Hear, hear!

POSTHUMUS.

Shall's have a play of this? Thou scornful page,

There lies thy part.

[Strikes her. She falls.]

PISANIO.

O gentlemen, help!

Mine and your mistress! O, my lord Posthumus!

You ne'er kill'd Imogen till now. Help, help!

Mine honour'd lady!

CYMBELINE.

Does the world go round?

POSTHUMUS.

How comes these staggers on me?

PISANIO.

Wake, my mistress!

CYMBELINE.

If this be so, the gods do mean to strike me

To death with mortal joy.

PISANIO.

How fares my mistress?

IMOGEN.

O, get thee from my sight;

Thou gav'st me poison. Dangerous fellow, hence!

Breathe not where princes are.

CYMBELINE.

The tune of Imogen!

PISANIO.

Lady,

The gods throw stones of sulphur on me, if

That box I gave you was not thought by me

A precious thing! I had it from the Queen.

CYMBELINE.

New matter still?

IMOGEN.

It poison'd me.

CORNELIUS.

O gods!

I left out one thing which the Queen confess'd,

Which must approve thee honest. 'If Pisanio

Have' said she 'given his mistress that confection

Which I gave him for cordial, she is serv'd

As I would serve a rat.'

CYMBELINE.

What's this, Cornelius?

CORNELIUS.

The Queen, sir, very oft importun'd me

To temper poisons for her; still pretending

The satisfaction of her knowledge only

In killing creatures vile, as cats and dogs,

Of no esteem. I, dreading that her purpose

Was of more danger, did compound for her

A certain stuff, which, being ta'en would cease

The present pow'r of life, but in short time

All offices of nature should again

Do their due functions. Have you ta'en of it?

IMOGEN.

Most like I did, for I was dead.

BELARIUS.

My boys,

There was our error.

GUIDERIUS.

This is sure Fidele.

IMOGEN.

Why did you throw your wedded lady from you?

Think that you are upon a rock, and now

Throw me again.

                                            [Embracing him.]

POSTHUMUS.

Hang there like fruit, my soul,

Till the tree die!

CYMBELINE.

How now, my flesh? my child?

What, mak'st thou me a dullard in this act?

Wilt thou not speak to me?

IMOGEN.

[Kneeling.] Your blessing, sir.

BELARIUS.

[To Guiderius and Arviragus.] Though you did love this youth, I blame ye not;

You had a motive for't.

CYMBELINE.

My tears that fall

Prove holy water on thee! Imogen,

Thy mother's dead.

IMOGEN.

I am sorry for't, my lord.

CYMBELINE.

O, she was naught, and long of her it was

That we meet here so strangely; but her son

Is gone, we know not how nor where.

PISANIO.

My lord,

Now fear is from me, I'll speak troth. Lord Cloten,

Upon my lady's missing, came to me

With his sword drawn, foam'd at the mouth, and swore,

If I discover'd not which way she was gone,

It was my instant death. By accident

I had a feigned letter of my master's

Then in my pocket, which directed him

To seek her on the mountains near to Milford;

Where, in a frenzy, in my master's garments,

Which he enforc'd from me, away he posts

With unchaste purpose, and with oath to violate

My lady's honour. What became of him

I further know not.

GUIDERIUS.

Let me end the story:

I slew him there.

CYMBELINE.

Marry, the gods forfend!

I would not thy good deeds should from my lips

Pluck a hard sentence. Prithee, valiant youth,

Deny't again.

GUIDERIUS.

I have spoke it, and I did it.

CYMBELINE.

He was a prince.

GUIDERIUS.

A most incivil one. The wrongs he did me

Were nothing prince-like; for he did provoke me

With language that would make me spurn the sea,

If it could so roar to me. I cut off's head,

And am right glad he is not standing here

To tell this tale of mine.

CYMBELINE.

I am sorry for thee.

By thine own tongue thou art condemn'd, and must

Endure our law. Thou'rt dead.

IMOGEN.

That headless man

I thought had been my lord.

CYMBELINE.

Bind the offender,

And take him from our presence.

BELARIUS.

Stay, sir King.

This man is better than the man he slew,

As well descended as thyself, and hath

More of thee merited than a band of Clotens

Had ever scar for. [To the guard.] Let his arms alone;

They were not born for bondage.

CYMBELINE.

Why, old soldier,

Wilt thou undo the worth thou art unpaid for

By tasting of our wrath? How of descent

As good as we?

ARVIRAGUS.

In that he spake too far.

CYMBELINE.

And thou shalt die for't.

BELARIUS.

We will die all three;

But I will prove that two on's are as good

As I have given out him. My sons, I must

For mine own part unfold a dangerous speech,

Though haply well for you.

ARVIRAGUS.

Your danger's ours.

GUIDERIUS.

And our good his.

BELARIUS.

Have at it then by leave!

Thou hadst, great King, a subject who

Was call'd Belarius.

CYMBELINE.

What of him? He is

A banish'd traitor.

BELARIUS.

He it is that hath

Assum'd this age; indeed a banish'd man;

I know not how a traitor.

CYMBELINE.

Take him hence,

The whole world shall not save him.

BELARIUS.

Not too hot.

First pay me for the nursing of thy sons,

And let it be confiscate all, so soon

As I have receiv'd it.

CYMBELINE.

Nursing of my sons?

BELARIUS.

I am too blunt and saucy: here's my knee.

Ere I arise I will prefer my sons;

Then spare not the old father. Mighty sir,

These two young gentlemen that call me father,

And think they are my sons, are none of mine;

They are the issue of your loins, my liege,

And blood of your begetting.

CYMBELINE.

How? my issue?

BELARIUS.

So sure as you your father's. I, old Morgan,

Am that Belarius whom you sometime banish'd.

Your pleasure was my mere offence, my punishment

Itself, and all my treason; that I suffer'd

Was all the harm I did. These gentle princes

(For such and so they are) these twenty years

Have I train'd up; those arts they have as I

Could put into them. My breeding was, sir, as

Your Highness knows. Their nurse, Euriphile,

Whom for the theft I wedded, stole these children

Upon my banishment; I mov'd her to't,

Having receiv'd the punishment before

For that which I did then. Beaten for loyalty

Excited me to treason. Their dear loss,

The more of you 'twas felt, the more it shap'd

Unto my end of stealing them. But, gracious sir,

Here are your sons again, and I must lose

Two of the sweet'st companions in the world.

The benediction of these covering heavens

Fall on their heads like dew! for they are worthy

To inlay heaven with stars.

CYMBELINE.

Thou weep'st and speak'st.

The service that you three have done is more

Unlike than this thou tell'st. I lost my children.

If these be they, I know not how to wish

A pair of worthier sons.

BELARIUS.

Be pleas'd awhile.

This gentleman, whom I call Polydore,

Most worthy prince, as yours, is true Guiderius;

This gentleman, my Cadwal, Arviragus,

Your younger princely son; he, sir, was lapp'd

In a most curious mantle, wrought by th' hand

Of his queen mother, which for more probation

I can with ease produce.

CYMBELINE.

Guiderius had

Upon his neck a mole, a sanguine star;

It was a mark of wonder.

BELARIUS.

This is he,

Who hath upon him still that natural stamp.

It was wise nature's end in the donation,

To be his evidence now.

CYMBELINE.

O, what am I?

A mother to the birth of three? Ne'er mother

Rejoic'd deliverance more. Blest pray you be,

That, after this strange starting from your orbs,

You may reign in them now! O Imogen,

Thou hast lost by this a kingdom.

IMOGEN.

No, my lord;

I have got two worlds by't. O my gentle brothers,

Have we thus met? O, never say hereafter

But I am truest speaker! You call'd me brother,

When I was but your sister: I you brothers,

When we were so indeed.

CYMBELINE.

Did you e'er meet?

ARVIRAGUS.

Ay, my good lord.

GUIDERIUS.

And at first meeting lov'd,

Continu'd so until we thought he died.

CORNELIUS.

By the Queen's dram she swallow'd.

CYMBELINE.

O rare instinct!

When shall I hear all through? This fierce abridgement

Hath to it circumstantial branches, which

Distinction should be rich in. Where? how liv'd you?

And when came you to serve our Roman captive?

How parted with your brothers? how first met them?

Why fled you from the court? and whither? These,

And your three motives to the battle, with

I know not how much more, should be demanded,

And all the other by-dependances,

From chance to chance; but nor the time nor place

Will serve our long interrogatories. See,

Posthumus anchors upon Imogen;

And she, like harmless lightning, throws her eye

On him, her brothers, me, her master, hitting

Each object with a joy; the counterchange

Is severally in all. Let's quit this ground,

And smoke the temple with our sacrifices.

[To Belarius.] Thou art my brother; so we'll hold thee ever.

IMOGEN.

You are my father too, and did relieve me

To see this gracious season.

CYMBELINE.

All o'erjoy'd

Save these in bonds. Let them be joyful too,

For they shall taste our comfort.

IMOGEN.

My good master,

I will yet do you service.

LUCIUS.

Happy be you!

CYMBELINE.

The forlorn soldier, that so nobly fought,

He would have well becom'd this place and grac'd

The thankings of a king.

POSTHUMUS.

I am, sir,

The soldier that did company these three

In poor beseeming; 'twas a fitment for

The purpose I then follow'd. That I was he,

Speak, Iachimo. I had you down, and might

Have made you finish.

IACHIMO.

[Kneeling.] I am down again;

But now my heavy conscience sinks my knee,

As then your force did. Take that life, beseech you,

Which I so often owe; but your ring first,

And here the bracelet of the truest princess

That ever swore her faith.

POSTHUMUS.

Kneel not to me.

The pow'r that I have on you is to spare you;

The malice towards you to forgive you. Live,

And deal with others better.

CYMBELINE.

Nobly doom'd!

We'll learn our freeness of a son-in-law;

Pardon's the word to all.

ARVIRAGUS.

You holp us, sir,

As you did mean indeed to be our brother;

Joy'd are we that you are.

POSTHUMUS.

Your servant, Princes. Good my lord of Rome,

Call forth your soothsayer. As I slept, methought

Great Jupiter, upon his eagle back'd,

Appear'd to me, with other spritely shows

Of mine own kindred. When I wak'd, I found

This label on my bosom; whose containing

Is so from sense in hardness that I can

Make no collection of it. Let him show

His skill in the construction.

LUCIUS.

Philarmonus!

SOOTHSAYER.

Here, my good lord.

LUCIUS.

Read, and declare the meaning.

SOOTHSAYER.

[Reads.] When as a lion's whelp shall, to himself unknown, without seeking find, and be embrac'd by a piece of tender air; and when from a stately cedar shall be lopp'd branches which, being dead many years, shall after revive, be jointed to the old stock, and freshly grow; then shall Posthumus end his miseries, Britain be fortunate and flourish in peace and plenty.

Thou, Leonatus, art the lion's whelp;

The fit and apt construction of thy name,

Being Leo-natus, doth import so much.

[To Cymbeline] The piece of tender air, thy virtuous daughter,

Which we call mollis aer, and mollis aer

We term it mulier; which mulier I divine

Is this most constant wife, who even now

Answering the letter of the oracle,

Unknown to you, unsought, were clipp'd about

With this most tender air.

CYMBELINE.

This hath some seeming.

SOOTHSAYER.

The lofty cedar, royal Cymbeline,

Personates thee; and thy lopp'd branches point

Thy two sons forth, who, by Belarius stol'n,

For many years thought dead, are now reviv'd,

To the majestic cedar join'd, whose issue

Promises Britain peace and plenty.

CYMBELINE.

Well,

My peace we will begin. And, Caius Lucius,

Although the victor, we submit to Cæsar

And to the Roman empire, promising

To pay our wonted tribute, from the which

We were dissuaded by our wicked queen,

Whom heavens in justice, both on her and hers,

Have laid most heavy hand.

SOOTHSAYER.

The fingers of the pow'rs above do tune

The harmony of this peace. The vision

Which I made known to Lucius ere the stroke

Of yet this scarce-cold battle, at this instant

Is full accomplish'd; for the Roman eagle,

From south to west on wing soaring aloft,

Lessen'd herself and in the beams o' th' sun

So vanish'd; which foreshow'd our princely eagle,

Th' imperial Cæsar, Cæsar, should again unite

His favour with the radiant Cymbeline,

Which shines here in the west.

CYMBELINE.

Laud we the gods;

And let our crooked smokes climb to their nostrils

From our bless'd altars. Publish we this peace

To all our subjects. Set we forward; let

A Roman and a British ensign wave

Friendly together. So through Lud's Town march;

And in the temple of great Jupiter

Our peace we'll ratify; seal it with feasts.

Set on there! Never was a war did cease,

Ere bloody hands were wash'd, with such a peace.

[Exeunt.]

363

About Author

Shakespeare produced most of his known works between 1589 and 1613. His early plays were primarily comedies and histories and are regarded as some of the best work produced in these genres. Until about 1608, he wrote mainly tragedies, among them Hamlet, Othello, King Lear, and Macbeth, all considered to be among the finest works in the English language. In the last phase of his life, he wrote tragicomedies (also known as romances) and collaborated with other playwrights.

Many of Shakespeare's plays were published in editions of varying quality and accuracy in his lifetime. However, in 1623, two fellow actors and friends of Shakespeare's, John Heminges and Henry Condell, published a more definitive text known as the First Folio, a posthumous collected edition of Shakespeare's dramatic works that included all but two of his plays. The volume was prefaced with a poem by Ben Jonson, in which Jonson presciently hails Shakespeare in a now-famous quote as "not of an age, but for all time".

Throughout the 20th and 21st centuries, Shakespeare's works have been continually adapted and rediscovered by new movements in scholarship and performance. His plays remain popular and are studied, performed, and reinterpreted through various cultural and political contexts around the world.

Early life

William Shakespeare was the son of John Shakespeare, an alderman and a successful glover (glove-maker) originally from Snitterfield, and Mary Arden, the daughter of an affluent landowning farmer. He was born in Stratford-upon-Avon and baptised there on 26 April 1564. His actual date of birth remains unknown, but is traditionally observed on 23 April, Saint George's Day. This date, which can be traced to a mistake made by an 18th-century scholar, has proved appealing to biographers because Shakespeare died on the same date in 1616. He was the third of eight children, and the eldest surviving son.

Although no attendance records for the period survive, most biographers agree that Shakespeare was probably educated at the King's New School in Stratford, a free school chartered in 1553, about a quarter-mile (400 m) from his home. Grammar schools varied in quality during the Elizabethan era, but grammar school curricula were largely similar: the basic Latin text was standardised by royal decree, and the school would have provided an intensive education in grammar based upon Latin classical authors.

At the age of 18, Shakespeare married 26-year-old Anne Hathaway. The consistory court of the Diocese of Worcester issued a marriage licence on 27 November 1582. The next day, two of Hathaway's neighbours posted bonds guaranteeing that no lawful claims impeded the marriage. The ceremony may have been arranged in some haste since the Worcester chancellor allowed the marriage banns to be read once instead of the usual three times, and six months after the marriage Anne gave birth to a daughter, Susanna, baptised 26 May 1583. Twins, son Hamnet and daughter Judith, followed almost two years later and were baptised 2 February 1585. Hamnet died of unknown causes at the age of 11 and was buried 11 August 1596.

After the birth of the twins, Shakespeare left few historical traces until he is mentioned as part of the London theatre scene in 1592. The exception is the appearance of his name in the "complaints bill" of a law case before the Queen's Bench court at Westminster dated Michaelmas Term 1588 and 9 October 1589. Scholars refer to the years between 1585 and 1592 as Shakespeare's "lost years". Biographers attempting to account for this period have reported many apocryphal stories. Nicholas Rowe, Shakespeare's first biographer, recounted a Stratford legend that Shakespeare fled the town for London to escape prosecution for deer poaching in the estate of local squire Thomas Lucy. Shakespeare is also supposed to have taken his revenge on Lucy by writing a scurrilous ballad about him. Another 18th-century story has Shakespeare starting his theatrical career minding the horses of theatre patrons in London. John Aubrey reported that Shakespeare had been a country schoolmaster. Some 20th-century scholars have suggested that Shakespeare may have been employed as a schoolmaster by Alexander

Hoghton of Lancashire, a Catholic landowner who named a certain "William Shakeshafte" in his will. Little evidence substantiates such stories other than hearsay collected after his death, and Shakeshafte was a common name in the Lancashire area.

London and theatrical career

It is not known definitively when Shakespeare began writing, but contemporary allusions and records of performances show that several of his plays were on the London stage by 1592. By then, he was sufficiently known in London to be attacked in print by the playwright Robert Greene in his Groats-Worth of Wit:

... there is an upstart Crow, beautified with our feathers, that with his Tiger's heart wrapped in a Player's hide, supposes he is as well able to bombast out a blank verse as the best of you: and being an absolute Johannes factotum, is in his own conceit the only Shake-scene in a country.

Scholars differ on the exact meaning of Greene's words, but most agree that Greene was accusing Shakespeare of reaching above his rank in trying to match such university-educated writers as Christopher Marlowe, Thomas Nashe, and Greene himself (the so-called "University Wits"). The italicised phrase parodying the line "Oh, tiger's heart wrapped in a woman's hide" from Shakespeare's Henry VI, Part 3, along with the pun "Shake-scene", clearly identify Shakespeare as Greene's target. As used here, Johannes Factotum ("Jack of all trades") refers to a second-rate tinkerer with the work of others, rather than the more common "universal genius".

Greene's attack is the earliest surviving mention of Shakespeare's work in the theatre. Biographers suggest that his career may have begun any time from the mid-1580s to just before Greene's remarks. After 1594, Shakespeare's plays were performed only by the Lord Chamberlain's Men, a company owned by a group of players, including Shakespeare, that soon became the leading playing company in London. After the death of Queen Elizabeth in 1603, the company was awarded a royal patent by the new King James I, and changed its name to the King's Men.

"All the world's a stage,

and all the men and women merely players:

they have their exits and their entrances;

and one man in his time plays many parts ..."

—As You Like It, Act II, Scene 7, 139–142

In 1599, a partnership of members of the company built their own theatre on the south bank of the River Thames, which they named the Globe. In 1608, the partnership also took over the Blackfriars indoor theatre. Extant records of Shakespeare's property purchases and investments indicate that his association with the company made him a wealthy man, and in 1597, he bought the second-largest house in Stratford, New Place, and in 1605, invested in a share of the parish tithes in Stratford.

Some of Shakespeare's plays were published in quarto editions, beginning in 1594, and by 1598, his name had become a selling point and began to appear on the title pages. Shakespeare continued to act in his own and other plays after his success as a playwright. The 1616 edition of Ben Jonson's Works names him on the cast lists for Every Man in His Humour (1598) and Sejanus His Fall (1603). The absence of his name from the 1605 cast list for Jonson's Volpone is taken by some scholars as a sign that his acting career was nearing its end. The First Folio of 1623, however, lists Shakespeare as one of "the Principal Actors in all these Plays", some of which were first staged after Volpone, although we cannot know for certain which roles he played. In 1610, John Davies of Hereford wrote that "good Will" played "kingly" roles. In 1709, Rowe passed down a tradition that Shakespeare played the ghost of Hamlet's father. Later traditions maintain that he also played Adam in As You Like It, and the Chorus in Henry V, though scholars doubt the sources of that information.

Throughout his career, Shakespeare divided his time between London and Stratford. In 1596, the year before he bought New Place as his family home in Stratford, Shakespeare was living in the parish of St. Helen's, Bishopsgate, north of the River Thames. He moved across the river to Southwark by 1599, the same year his company constructed the Globe Theatre there. By 1604, he had moved north of the river again, to an area north of St Paul's Cathedral with many fine houses. There, he rented rooms from a French Huguenot named Christopher Mountjoy, a maker of ladies' wigs and other headgear.

Later years and death

Rowe was the first biographer to record the tradition, repeated by Johnson, that Shakespeare retired to Stratford "some years before his death". He was still working as an actor in London in 1608; in an answer to the sharers' petition in 1635, Cuthbert Burbage stated that after purchasing the lease of the Blackfriars Theatre in 1608 from Henry Evans, the King's Men "placed men players" there, "which were Heminges, Condell, Shakespeare, etc.". However, it is perhaps relevant that the bubonic plague raged in London throughout 1609. The London public playhouses were repeatedly closed during extended outbreaks of the plague (a total of over 60 months closure between May 1603 and February 1610), which meant there was often no acting work. Retirement from all work was uncommon at that time. Shakespeare continued to visit London during the years 1611–1614. In 1612, he was called as a witness in Bellott v. Mountjoy, a court case concerning the marriage settlement of Mountjoy's daughter, Mary. In March 1613, he bought a gatehouse in the former Blackfriars priory; and from November 1614, he was in London for several weeks with his son-in-law, John Hall. After 1610, Shakespeare wrote fewer plays, and none are attributed to him after 1613. His last three plays were collaborations, probably with John Fletcher, who succeeded him as the house playwright of the King's Men.

Shakespeare died on 23 April 1616, at the age of 52. He died within a month of signing his will, a document which he begins by describing himself as being in "perfect health". No extant contemporary source explains how or why he died. Half a century later, John Ward, the vicar of Stratford, wrote in his notebook: "Shakespeare, Drayton, and Ben Jonson had a merry meeting and, it seems, drank too hard, for Shakespeare died of a fever there contracted", not an impossible scenario since Shakespeare knew Jonson and Drayton. Of the tributes from fellow authors, one refers to his relatively sudden death: "We wondered, Shakespeare, that thou went'st so soon / From the world's stage to the grave's tiring room."

He was survived by his wife and two daughters. Susanna had married a physician, John Hall, in 1607, and Judith had married Thomas Quiney, a vintner, two months before Shakespeare's death. Shakespeare signed his last will and testament on 25 March 1616; the following day, his new son-in-law, Thomas Quiney was found guilty of fathering an illegitimate son by Margaret Wheeler, who had died during childbirth. Thomas was ordered by the church court to do public penance, which would have caused much shame and embarrassment for the Shakespeare family.

Shakespeare bequeathed the bulk of his large estate to his elder daughter Susanna under stipulations that she pass it down intact to "the first son of her body". The Quineys had three children, all of whom died without marrying. The Halls had one child, Elizabeth, who married twice but died without children in 1670, ending Shakespeare's direct line. Shakespeare's will scarcely mentions his wife, Anne, who was probably entitled to one-third of his estate automatically. He did make a point, however, of leaving her "my second best bed", a bequest that has led to much speculation. Some scholars see the bequest as an insult to Anne, whereas others believe that the second-best bed would have been the matrimonial bed and therefore rich in significance.

Shakespeare was buried in the chancel of the Holy Trinity Church two days after his death. The epitaph carved into the stone slab covering his grave includes a curse against moving his bones, which was carefully avoided during restoration of the church in 2008:

Good frend for Iesvs sake forbeare,

To digg the dvst encloased heare.

Bleste be Middle English the.svg man Middle English that.svg spares thes stones,

And cvrst be he Middle English that.svg moves my bones.

(Modern spelling: Good friend, for Jesus' sake forbear, / To dig the dust enclosed here. / Blessed be the man that spares these stones, / And cursed be he that moves my bones.)

Some time before 1623, a funerary monument was erected in his memory on the north wall, with a half-effigy of him in the act of writing. Its plaque compares him to Nestor, Socrates, and Virgil. In 1623, in conjunction with the publication of the First Folio, the Droeshout engraving was published.

Shakespeare has been commemorated in many statues and memorials around the world, including funeral monuments in Southwark Cathedral and Poets' Corner in Westminster Abbey.

Plays

Most playwrights of the period typically collaborated with others at some point, and critics agree that Shakespeare did the same, mostly early and late in his career. Some attributions, such as Titus Andronicus and the early history plays, remain controversial while The Two Noble Kinsmen and the lost Cardenio have well-attested contemporary documentation. Textual evidence also supports the view that several of the plays were revised by other writers after their original composition.

The first recorded works of Shakespeare are Richard III and the three parts of Henry VI, written in the early 1590s during a vogue for historical drama. Shakespeare's plays are difficult to date precisely, however, and studies of the texts suggest that Titus Andronicus, The Comedy of Errors, The Taming of the Shrew, and The Two Gentlemen of Verona may also belong to Shakespeare's earliest period. His first histories, which draw heavily on the 1587 edition of Raphael Holinshed's Chronicles of England, Scotland, and Ireland, dramatise the destructive results of weak or corrupt rule and have been interpreted as a justification for the origins of the Tudor dynasty. The early plays were influenced by the works of other Elizabethan dramatists, especially Thomas Kyd and Christopher Marlowe, by the traditions of medieval drama, and by the plays of Seneca. The Comedy of Errors was also based on classical models, but no source for The Taming of the Shrew has been found, though it is related to a separate play of the same name and may have derived from a folk story. Like The Two Gentlemen of Verona, in which two friends appear to approve of rape, the Shrew's story of the taming of a woman's independent spirit by a man sometimes troubles modern critics, directors, and audiences.

Shakespeare's early classical and Italianate comedies, containing tight double plots and precise comic sequences, give way in the mid-1590s to the romantic atmosphere of his most acclaimed comedies. A Midsummer Night's Dream is a witty mixture of romance, fairy magic, and comic lowlife scenes. Shakespeare's next comedy, the equally romantic Merchant of Venice, contains a portrayal of the vengeful Jewish moneylender Shylock, which reflects Elizabethan views but may appear derogatory to modern audiences. The wit and wordplay of Much Ado About Nothing, the charming rural setting of As You Like It, and the lively merrymaking of Twelfth Night complete Shakespeare's sequence of great comedies. After the lyrical Richard II, written almost entirely in verse, Shakespeare introduced prose comedy into the histories of the late 1590s, Henry IV, parts 1 and 2, and Henry V. His characters become more complex and tender as he switches deftly between comic and serious scenes, prose and poetry, and achieves the narrative variety of his mature work. This period begins and ends with two tragedies: Romeo and Juliet, the famous romantic tragedy of sexually charged adolescence, love, and death; and Julius Caesar—based on Sir Thomas North's 1579 translation of Plutarch's Parallel Lives—which introduced a new kind of drama. According to Shakespearean scholar James Shapiro, in Julius Caesar, "the various strands of politics, character, inwardness, contemporary events, even Shakespeare's own reflections on the act of writing, began to infuse each other".

In the early 17th century, Shakespeare wrote the so-called "problem plays" Measure for Measure, Troilus and Cressida, and All's Well That Ends Well and a number of his best known tragedies. Many critics believe that Shakespeare's greatest tragedies represent the peak of his art. The titular hero of one of Shakespeare's greatest tragedies, Hamlet, has probably been discussed more than any other Shakespearean character, especially for his famous soliloquy which begins "To be or not to be; that is the question". Unlike the introverted Hamlet, whose fatal flaw is hesitation, the heroes of the tragedies that followed, Othello and King Lear, are undone by hasty errors of judgement. The plots of Shakespeare's tragedies often hinge on such fatal errors or flaws, which overturn order and destroy the hero and those he loves. In Othello, the villain Iago stokes Othello's sexual jealousy to the point where he murders the innocent wife who loves him. In King Lear, the old king commits the tragic error of giving up his powers, initiating the events which lead to the torture and blinding of the Earl of Gloucester and the murder of Lear's youngest daughter Cordelia. According to the critic Frank Kermode, "the play-offers neither its good characters nor its audience any relief from its cruelty". In Macbeth, the shortest and most compressed of Shakespeare's tragedies, uncontrollable ambition incites Macbeth and his wife, Lady Macbeth, to murder the rightful king and usurp the throne until their own guilt destroys them in turn. In this play, Shakespeare adds a supernatural element to the tragic structure. His last major tragedies, Antony and Cleopatra and Coriolanus, contain some of Shakespeare's finest poetry and were considered his most successful tragedies by the poet and critic T.S. Eliot.

In his final period, Shakespeare turned to romance or tragicomedy and completed three more major plays: Cymbeline, The Winter's Tale, and The Tempest, as well as the collaboration, Pericles, Prince of Tyre. Less bleak than the tragedies, these four plays are graver in tone than the comedies of the 1590s, but they end with reconciliation and the forgiveness of potentially tragic errors. Some commentators have seen this change in mood as evidence of a more serene view of life on Shakespeare's part, but it may merely reflect the theatrical fashion of the day. Shakespeare collaborated on two further surviving plays, Henry VIII and The Two Noble Kinsmen, probably with John Fletcher.

Performances

It is not clear for which companies Shakespeare wrote his early plays. The title page of the 1594 edition of Titus Andronicus reveals that the play had been acted by three different troupes. After the plagues of 1592–3, Shakespeare's plays were performed by his own company at The Theatre and the Curtain in Shoreditch, north of the Thames. Londoners flocked there to see the first part of Henry IV, Leonard Digges recording, "Let but Falstaff come, Hal, Poins, the rest ... and you scarce shall have a room". When the company found themselves in dispute with their landlord, they pulled The

Theatre down and used the timbers to construct the Globe Theatre, the first playhouse built by actors for actors, on the south bank of the Thames at Southwark. The Globe opened in autumn 1599, with Julius Caesar one of the first plays staged. Most of Shakespeare's greatest post-1599 plays were written for the Globe, including Hamlet, Othello, and King Lear.

After the Lord Chamberlain's Men were renamed the King's Men in 1603, they entered a special relationship with the new King James. Although the performance records are patchy, the King's Men performed seven of Shakespeare's plays at court between 1 November 1604, and 31 October 1605, including two performances of The Merchant of Venice. After 1608, they performed at the indoor Blackfriars Theatre during the winter and the Globe during the summer. The indoor setting, combined with the Jacobean fashion for lavishly staged masques, allowed Shakespeare to introduce more elaborate stage devices. In Cymbeline, for example, Jupiter descends "in thunder and lightning, sitting upon an eagle: he throws a thunderbolt. The ghosts fall on their knees."

The actors in Shakespeare's company included the famous Richard Burbage, William Kempe, Henry Condell and John Heminges. Burbage played the leading role in the first performances of many of Shakespeare's plays, including Richard III, Hamlet, Othello, and King Lear. The popular comic actor Will Kempe played the servant Peter in Romeo and Juliet and Dogberry in Much Ado About Nothing, among other characters. He was replaced around 1600 by Robert Armin, who played roles such as Touchstone in As You Like It and the fool in King Lear. In 1613, Sir Henry Wotton recorded that Henry VIII "was set forth with many extraordinary circumstances of pomp and ceremony". On 29 June, however, a cannon set fire to the thatch of the Globe and burned the theatre to the ground, an event which pinpoints the date of a Shakespeare play with rare precision.

Textual sources

In 1623, John Heminges and Henry Condell, two of Shakespeare's friends from the King's Men, published the First Folio, a collected edition of Shakespeare's plays. It contained 36 texts, including 18 printed for the first time. Many of the plays had already appeared in quarto versions—flimsy books made from sheets of paper folded twice to make four leaves. No evidence suggests that Shakespeare approved these editions, which the First Folio describes as "stol'n and surreptitious copies". Nor did Shakespeare plan or expect his works to survive in any form at all; those works likely would have faded into oblivion but for his friends' spontaneous idea, after his death, to create and publish the First Folio.

Alfred Pollard termed some of the pre-1623 versions as "bad quartos" because of their adapted, paraphrased or garbled texts, which may in places have been reconstructed from memory. Where several versions of a play survive, each differs from the other. The differences may stem from copying or printing errors, from notes by actors or audience members, or from Shakespeare's own papers. In some cases, for example, Hamlet, Troilus and Cressida, and Othello, Shakespeare could have revised the texts between the quarto and folio editions. In the case of King Lear, however, while most modern editions do conflate them, the 1623 folio version is so different from the 1608 quarto that the Oxford Shakespeare prints them both, arguing that they cannot be conflated without confusion.

Influence from neighbours in London

Ten years of research by Geoffrey Marsh (museum director) of the Victoria and Albert Museum in London may have shown that Shakespeare got many of the ideas and information for his plays, from his neighbours that he lived near in London in the late 1590s.

Geoffrey Marsh found the site of Shakespeare's house in St Helen's Church, Bishopsgate parish, at the corner of St.Helen's churchyard and Bishopsgate Street, north of the churchyard, from the records of the Leathersellers Company. Many wealthy and notable people (including Sir John Spencer and Dr. Edward Jorden and Dr. Peter Turner), with connections across Europe, lived near Shakespeare.

Poems

In 1593 and 1594, when the theatres were closed because of plague,

Shakespeare published two narrative poems on sexual themes, Venus and Adonis and The Rape of Lucrece. He dedicated them to Henry Wriothesley, Earl of Southampton. In Venus and Adonis, an innocent Adonis rejects the sexual advances of Venus; while in The Rape of Lucrece, the virtuous wife Lucrece is raped by the lustful Tarquin. Influenced by Ovid's Metamorphoses, the poems show the guilt and moral confusion that result from uncontrolled lust. Both proved popular and were often reprinted during Shakespeare's lifetime. A third narrative poem, A Lover's Complaint, in which a young woman laments her seduction by a persuasive suitor, was printed in the first edition of the Sonnets in 1609. Most scholars now accept that Shakespeare wrote A Lover's Complaint. Critics consider that its fine qualities are marred by leaden effects. The Phoenix and the Turtle, printed in Robert Chester's 1601 Love's Martyr, mourns the deaths of the legendary phoenix and his lover, the faithful turtle dove. In 1599, two early drafts of sonnets 138 and 144 appeared in The Passionate Pilgrim, published under Shakespeare's name but without his permission.

Sonnets

Published in 1609, the Sonnets were the last of Shakespeare's non-dramatic works to be printed. Scholars are not certain when each of the 154 sonnets was composed, but evidence suggests that Shakespeare wrote sonnets throughout his career for a private readership. Even before the two unauthorised sonnets appeared in The Passionate Pilgrim in 1599, Francis Meres had referred in 1598 to Shakespeare's "sugred Sonnets among his private friends". Few analysts believe that the published collection follows Shakespeare's intended sequence. He seems to have planned two contrasting series: one about uncontrollable lust for a married woman of dark complexion (the "dark lady"), and one about conflicted love for a fair young man (the "fair youth"). It remains unclear if these figures represent real individuals, or if the authorial "I" who addresses them represents Shakespeare himself, though Wordsworth believed that with the sonnets "Shakespeare unlocked his heart"

"Shall I compare thee to a summer's day?

Thou art more lovely and more temperate ..."

—Lines from Shakespeare's Sonnet 18.

The 1609 edition was dedicated to a "Mr. W.H.", credited as "the only begetter" of the poems. It is not known whether this was written by Shakespeare himself or by the publisher, Thomas Thorpe, whose initials appear at the foot of the dedication page; nor is it known who Mr. W.H. was, despite numerous theories, or whether Shakespeare even authorised the publication. Critics praise the Sonnets as a profound meditation on the nature of love, sexual passion, procreation, death, and time.

Style

Shakespeare's first plays were written in the conventional style of the day. He wrote them in a stylised language that does not always spring naturally from the needs of the characters or the drama. The poetry depends on extended, sometimes elaborate metaphors and conceits, and the language is often rhetorical—written for actors to declaim rather than speak. The grand speeches in Titus Andronicus, in the view of some critics, often hold up the action, for example; and the verse in The Two Gentlemen of Verona has been described as stilted.

However, Shakespeare soon began to adapt the traditional styles to his own purposes. The opening soliloquy of Richard III has its roots in the self-declaration of Vice in medieval drama. At the same time, Richard's vivid self-awareness looks forward to the soliloquies of Shakespeare's mature plays. No single play marks a change from the traditional to the freer style. Shakespeare combined the two throughout his career, with Romeo and Juliet perhaps the best example of the mixing of the styles. By the time of Romeo and Juliet, Richard II, and A Midsummer Night's Dream in the mid-1590s, Shakespeare had begun to write a more natural poetry. He increasingly tuned his metaphors and images to the needs of the drama itself.

Shakespeare's standard poetic form was blank verse, composed in iambic pentameter. In practice, this meant that his verse was usually unrhymed and consisted of ten syllables to a line, spoken with a stress on every second syllable. The blank verse of his early plays is quite different from that of his later ones. It is often beautiful, but its sentences tend to start, pause, and finish at the end of lines, with the risk of monotony. Once Shakespeare mastered traditional blank verse, he began to interrupt and vary its flow. This technique releases the new power and flexibility of the poetry in plays such as Julius Caesar and Hamlet. Shakespeare uses it, for example, to convey the turmoil in Hamlet's mind:

> Sir, in my heart there was a kind of fighting
>
> That would not let me sleep. Methought I lay
>
> Worse than the mutines in the bilboes. Rashly—
>
> And prais'd be rashness for it—let us know
>
> Our indiscretion sometimes serves us well ...
>
> —Hamlet, Act 5, Scene 2, 4–8

After Hamlet, Shakespeare varied his poetic style further, particularly in the more emotional passages of the late tragedies. The literary critic A. C. Bradley described this style as "more concentrated, rapid, varied, and, in construction, less regular, not seldom twisted or elliptical". In the last phase of his career, Shakespeare adopted many techniques to achieve these effects. These included run-on lines, irregular pauses and stops, and extreme variations in sentence structure and length. In Macbeth, for example, the language darts from one unrelated metaphor or simile to another: "was the hope drunk/ Wherein you dressed yourself?" (1.7.35–38); "... pity, like a naked new-born babe/ Striding the blast, or heaven's cherubim, hors'd/ Upon the sightless couriers of the air ..." (1.7.21–25). The listener is challenged to complete the sense. The late romances, with their shifts in time and surprising turns of plot, inspired a last poetic style in which long and short sentences are set against one another, clauses are piled up, subject and object are reversed, and words are omitted, creating an effect of spontaneity.

Shakespeare combined poetic genius with a practical sense of the theatre. Like all playwrights of the time, he dramatised stories from sources such as Plutarch and Holinshed. He reshaped each plot to create several centres of interest and to show as many sides of a narrative to the audience as possible. This strength of design ensures that a Shakespeare play can survive translation, cutting and wide interpretation without loss to its core drama. As Shakespeare's mastery grew, he gave his characters clearer and more varied motivations and distinctive patterns of speech. He preserved aspects of his earlier style in the later plays, however. In Shakespeare's late romances, he deliberately returned to a more artificial style, which emphasised the illusion of theatre.

Influence

Shakespeare's work has made a lasting impression on later theatre and literature. In particular, he expanded the dramatic potential of characterisation, plot, language, and genre. Until Romeo and Juliet, for example, romance had not been viewed as a worthy topic for tragedy. Soliloquies had been used mainly to convey information about characters or events, but Shakespeare used them to explore characters' minds. His work heavily influenced later poetry. The Romantic poets attempted to revive Shakespearean verse drama, though with little success. Critic George Steiner described all English verse dramas from Coleridge to Tennyson as "feeble variations on Shakespearean themes."

Shakespeare influenced novelists such as Thomas Hardy, William Faulkner, and Charles Dickens. The American novelist Herman Melville's soliloquies owe much to Shakespeare; his Captain Ahab in Moby-Dick is a classic tragic hero, inspired by King Lear. Scholars have identified 20,000 pieces of music linked to Shakespeare's works. These include three operas by Giuseppe Verdi, Macbeth, Otello and Falstaff, whose critical standing compares with that of the source plays. Shakespeare has also inspired many painters, including the Romantics and the Pre-Raphaelites. The Swiss Romantic artist Henry Fuseli, a friend of William Blake, even translated Macbeth into German. The psychoanalyst Sigmund Freud drew on Shakespearean psychology, in particular, that of Hamlet, for his theories of human nature.

In Shakespeare's day, English grammar, spelling, and pronunciation were less standardised than they are now, and his use of language helped shape

379

modern English. Samuel Johnson quoted him more often than any other author in his A Dictionary of the English Language, the first serious work of its type. Expressions such as "with bated breath" (Merchant of Venice) and "a foregone conclusion" (Othello) have found their way into everyday English speech.

Works

Classification of the plays

Shakespeare's works include the 36 plays printed in the First Folio of 1623, listed according to their folio classification as comedies, histories, and tragedies. Two plays not included in the First Folio, The Two Noble Kinsmen and Pericles, Prince of Tyre, are now accepted as part of the canon, with today's scholars agreeing that Shakespeare made major contributions to the writing of both. No Shakespearean poems were included in the First Folio.

In the late 19th century, Edward Dowden classified four of the late comedies as romances, and though many scholars prefer to call them tragicomedies, Dowden's term is often used. In 1896, Frederick S. Boas coined the term "problem plays" to describe four plays: All's Well That Ends Well, Measure for Measure, Troilus and Cressida, and Hamlet. "Dramas as singular in theme and temper cannot be strictly called comedies or tragedies", he wrote. "We may, therefore, borrow a convenient phrase from the theatre of today and class them together as Shakespeare's problem plays." The term, much debated and sometimes applied to other plays, remains in use, though Hamlet is definitively classed as a tragedy. (Source: Wikipedia)

CPSIA information can be obtained
at www.ICGtesting.com
Printed in the USA
BVHW031321160919
558489BV00002BA/469/P